T0017073

WHAT IS LIFE? Edited by Biogroop in association with Katrin Klingan and Nick Houde, with contributions by Stefan Helmreich, Evelyn Fox Keller, Natasha Myers, Sophia Roosth, and Michael Rossi

What Is Life?

Edited by
Stefan Helmreich, Natasha Myers, Sophia Roosth,
and Michael Rossi (Biogroop)

in association with
Katrin Klingan and Nick Houde

Sister.
The Vitality
of your Syllables
compensates
for their
infrequency.
There is not
so much Life
as Talk of
Life, as a
general thing.
Had we the
first intimation
of the Definition
of Life, the
Calmest of us

Contents

Foreword

"What is life?" This is exactly the kind of question that, once asked, leads to a flood of vexing problems, whether in biology, technology, or governance. But it is also the sort of question that rolls back to reveal the epistemological investments of those who pose it. How it is answered can disclose commitments to methods of inquiry as well as ideological assumptions about matters of origin, value, and futurity.

This book emerged out of conversations following a multiyear research initiative at HKW that focused on the technosphere—the material and temporal sphere formed by the growing interconnectedness of human culture, natural environments, and planetary-scale technologies. It became clear that understanding the technosphere means investigating the relationships between life and the forms it takes and enables. The extent to which technology has irrevocably altered the conditions of existence on the planet forms a new context for the genesis of novel forms of social and cultural life and, in doing so, changes how we understand life forms themselves.

This realization led us to the essay "Life Forms: A Keyword Entry," authored by anthropologists of biology Sophia Roosth and Stefan Helmreich, published in *Representations* in 2010. The article builds a historical account of the term "life form" as it has developed over the last few centuries of Western natural philosophy and biology. Roosth and Helmreich use the term to investigate the scientific and philosophical assumptions behind life science and, in so doing, invite the reader to speculate about what life forms have been and might yet be.

The present book is the product of the collaborative effort of Biogroop, bringing Roosth and Helmreich together with anthropologist of science Natasha Myers and historian of science Michael Rossi. The work maps out how the question "What is life?" has been posed in various contexts since the nineteenth century. The book collects an archive of journal articles that host the question in their title. The one or two page selections from these pieces trace how different disciplines have articulated the connection between life and form over the past century, unfurling the many implicit ideologies and presuppositions that have shaped answers to the query. As the notion of life itself gets stranger and more difficult to pin down, the selections—and the Biogroop collective—open up possibilities about how this connection might be conceived in the future.

Within the broader ambit of the publication series *DNA–Das Neue Alphabet* (The New Alphabet), we see the compilation of this archive and the contributions in this book as an exemplary method for elucidating the epistemic scaffolds that underlie the concepts employed in making sense of the universe. In this way, the volume speaks to the central concept of the series: to explore the ordering systems of knowledge by unfolding the representations, concepts, and methods that make them possible.

The new ways of making these knowledge systems operational afford new possibilities for their use. This entails using them not just as representational forms, but also as tools—similar to the way alphabets operate within language. These tools, in turn, inscribe modes of representations into physical things in order to manipulate them and produce unforeseen combinations. Used in this way, such representations expand what is known by questioning what could be.

Thinking about knowledge in such a manner produces a number of political and ethical questions. If one is no longer shackled to the known world, then what possible worlds, what possible re-combinations, are worth searching for? Is it simply about making something new and thus expanding an overall understanding of the cosmos? Or, would forms of thought benefit from being further qualified by their underlying motivations, such as utility, general well-being, discernment, or justice—all of which ultimately guide how operational knowledge came about in the first place?

The long-term collaboration by Biogroop that has produced this archive provides a rich pathway through knowledge systems, and we are pleased that they have accepted the invitation to publish an articulation of their project as part of the *DNA* series.

Katrin Klingan, Nick Houde

What Is Life?

In his programmatic, discipline-dubbing 1802 text *Biologie*, Gottfried Treviranus asked "What is life?"—a question that has impelled many life science texts since.[1] So, for example, in 1944, physicist Erwin Schrödinger famously published *What Is Life?*—a compact book which suggested that physics might supply an answer to the question. Schrödinger hypothesized that "life" might be carried by the structure of an aperiodic crystal, a form capable, he argued, of containing and executing a set of instructions for making an organism, instructions which, transmitted from one generation to the next, could survive a world characterized by entropy, that inescapable entailment of the second law of thermodynamics. Schrödinger offered that such a crystal might contain a "code-script" of life, and something like its structure was later discerned in the nucleotide sequence-bearing armature of the double helix of DNA (deoxyribonucleic acid).[2] In 1995, biologist Lynn Margulis and her son, Dorion Sagan, advanced a less reductionist, less unitary definition in their own *What Is Life?*. In that book, Margulis and Sagan delivered iterative and looping answers to the question for each of life's five kingdoms: bacteria, protists, animals, fungi, and plants. After having been compressed by Schrödinger into the linear logic of a code, "life" emerged for Margulis and Sagan as an efflorescence of bodied forms.[3] These are only the most notable data points in the pastime of asking "What is life?." If one placed end-to-end all the various texts entitled *What Is Life?*—throwing in Augusta Gaskell's 1928 *What Is Life?*, J.B.S. Haldane's 1947 *What Is Life?*, Fritjof Capra and Pier Luigi Luisi's 2014 "What is life?" for good measure[4]—one might find the concatenation

1   Gottfried Reinhold Treviranus, *Biologie, oder, Philosophie der lebenden Natur für Naturforscher und Aerzte.* Göttingen: Bey J. F. Röwer, 1802, p. 16.
2   Erwin Schrödinger, *What Is Life? The Physical Aspect of the Living Cell.* Cambridge: Cambridge University Press, 1944.
3   Lynn Margulis and Dorion Sagan, *What Is Life?.* Berkeley, CA: University of California Press, 1995.
4   Augusta Gaskell, *What is Life?.* Springfield, IL: Charles C. Thomas, 1928; J. B. S. Haldane, *What Is Life?.* New York: Boni and Gaer, 1947; Fritjof Capra and Pier Luigi Luisi, "What is life?," in Fritjof Capra and Pier Luigi Luisi, *The Systems View of Life: A Unifying Vision.* Cambridge: Cambridge University Press, 2014.

to read something like a chain of morphing refrains, moving through accounts of "life" as manifesting in biocrystalline pattern, as unfolding through code and information, as recursively animating systems of self-contained and self-generating processes (*autopoiesis*), and as ever-entangled across kingdoms in symbiotic, planet-wide relation and realization (*sympoiesis*).[5]

If Schrödinger addressed the "What is life?" question from the vantage of a physicist and Margulis and Sagan treated it from the domain of the biological sciences, by the turn of the millennium, historians, philosophers, rhetoricians, anthropologists, cultural and media theorists, and many others had started to think reflexively about it, working to contextualize the arrival and form of posing the question itself. They took as their inspiration a formulation of Michel Foucault's from *The Order of Things*:

> Historians want to write histories of biology in the eighteenth century; but they do not realize that biology did not exist then, and that the pattern of knowledge that has been familiar to us for a hundred and fifty years is not valid for a previous period. And that, if biology was unknown, there was a very

5   On *autopoiesis*, see Humberto R. Maturana and Francisco J. Varela, *Autopoiesis and Cognition: The Realization of the Living* (Boston Studies in the Philosophy and History of Science). Dordrecht: Reidel, 1972. For an intriguing foreshadowing of *autopoiesis* as self-making, consider Friedrich Engels' definition of life: "*Life is the mode of existence of albuminous bodies*, and this mode of existence essentially consists in the constant self-renewal of the chemical constituents of these bodies." Quoted from Friedrich Engels, *Anti-Dühring: Herr Eugen Dühring's Revolution in Science*, trans. Emile Burns from the 1894 German edition of *Herrn Eugen Dührings Umwälzung der Wissenschaft* (Leipzig, 1878). See Moscow: Progress Press, 1947, https://www.marxists.org/archive/marx/works/1877/anti-duhring/ch06.htm, accessed April 27, 2021. On *sympoiesis* see Beth Dempster, "Sympoietic and Autopoietic Systems: A New Distinction for Self-Organizing Systems," paper presented at the Proceedings of the World Congress of the System Sciences and ISSS, 2000, Toronto, Canada. See pdf-version, https://citeseerx.ist.psu.edu/viewdoc/download?doi=10.1.1.582.1177&rep=rep1&type=pdf, accessed April 29, 2021; Donna Haraway, "Sympoiesis: Symbiogenesis and the Lively Arts of Staying with the Trouble," in Donna Haraway, *Staying with the Trouble: Making Kin in the Chthulucene*. Durham, NC: Duke University Press, 2016, pp. 58–98.

simple reason for it: that life itself did not exist. All that existed was living beings, which were viewed through a grid of knowledge constituted by *natural history*.[6]

Thus, historians chronicled how the notion of the gene came to be understood as an agent and token for the "life" traced in Darwin's account of evolution by natural selection. They examined how the genetic "code" as a proxy for life came to be contoured by language from twentieth-century cryptography, computer programming, and data science, eventually shaping the emergence of genomics as an information science—even as the info-idiom never quite shook off its inheritance of Aristotelian and preformationist visions of vitality as the result of form imprinted on matter.[7] Alongside this story, other historians tracked how cell biology and its culture media never quite yielded fully to talk of life as information.[8] Philosophers and

6   Michel Foucault, *Les Mots et les choses: Une archéologie des sciences humaines*. Paris: Éditions Gallimard, 1966; trans. Alan Sheridan, *The Order of Things: An Archaeology of the Human Sciences*. New York: Pantheon Books, 1970, pp. 127–28.

7   Evelyn Fox Keller, *Refiguring Life: Metaphors of Twentieth-Century Biology*. New York: Columbia University Press, 1995; Lily Kay, *Who Wrote the Book of Life? A History of the Genetic Code*. Stanford, CA: Stanford University Press, 2000; Evelyn Fox Keller, *The Century of the Gene*. Cambridge, MA: MIT Press, 2000; Soraya de Chadarevian, *Designs for Life: Molecular Biology after World War II*. Cambridge: Cambridge University Press, 2000; Evelyn Fox Keller, *Making Sense of Life: Explaining Biological Development with Models, Metaphors, and Machines*. Cambridge, MA: Harvard University Press, 2002; Phillip Thurtle, *The Emergence of Genetic Rationality*. Seattle, WA: University of Washington Press, 2008; Hallam Stevens, *Life Out of Sequence: A Data-Driven History of Bioinformatics*. Chicago, IL: University of Chicago Press, 2013; Hans-Jörg Rheinberger, *The Gene: From Genetics to Postgenomics*. Chicago, IL: University of Chicago Press, 2018; Bruno J. Strasser, *Collecting Experiments: Making Big Data Biology*. Chicago, IL: University of Chicago Press, 2018; Mathias Grote, *Membranes to Molecular Machines: Active Matter and the Remaking of Life*. Chicago, IL: University of Chicago Press, 2019.

8   Hannah Landecker, *Culturing Life: How Cells Became Technologies*. Cambridge, MA: Harvard University Press, 2007; Maureen A. O'Malley and Staffan Müller-Wille, "The Cell as Nexus: Connections between the History, Philosophy and Science of Cell Biology," *Studies in History and Philosophy of Science Part C: Studies in History and Philosophy of Biological and Biomedical Sciences*, vol. 41, no. 3 (2010), pp. 169–71.

rhetoricians, meanwhile, tracked how vitalist and metaphysical rhetoric seemed always to haunt biology, even at its most reductionist (and, sometimes, too, at its most holist).[9] In anthropology and cultural studies, scholars diagnosed the ways sex/gender, reproduction, sexuality, race, and capital conditioned descriptions of "life itself" as, variously, a self-creating (and self-referential) principle of paternal origination and seminal invention, a newly cybernetic amalgam of informatic and biological reason, a code-script for purity and divergence in racialized replication, and a taxonomic frame for securing property claims in organic things.[10] In more recent science studies, "life" came to be recognized as bound up not only with the politics and economics of biology, but also with transformations of bodies and ecologies damaged by corporate chemistry, often through the dumping and distributions of toxins into the environment[11]—formations of what historian Michelle Murphy has called "alterlife," themselves built upon *longue durée* dispossessions of land and livelihood from

---

9   Richard Doyle, *On Beyond Living: Rhetorical Transformations of the Life Sciences*. Stanford, CA: Stanford University Press, 1997; Keith Ansell Pearson, *Viroid Life: Perspectives on Nietzsche and the Transhuman Condition*. London: Routledge, 1997; N. Katherine Hayles, *How We Became Posthuman: Virtual Bodies in Cybernetics, Literature and Informatics*. Chicago, IL: University of Chicago Press, 1999; Susan Oyama, *The Ontogeny of Information: Developmental Systems and Evolution*, 2nd rev. exp. ed. Durham, NC: Duke University Press, 2000; Anneke Smelik and Nina Lykke, *Bits of Life: Feminism at the Intersection of Media, Bioscience, and Technology*. Seattle, WA: University of Washington Press, 2008; Eugene Thacker, *After Life*. Chicago, IL: University of Chicago Press, 2010; Thierry Bardini, *Junkware*. Minneapolis, MN: University of Minnesota Press, 2011; Sabina Leonelli, *Data-Centric Biology: A Philosophical Study*. Chicago, IL: University of Chicago Press, 2016.

10 Marilyn Strathern, *Reproducing the Future: Anthropology, Kinship, and the New Reproductive Technologies*. New York: Routledge, 1992; Donna Haraway, *Modest_Witness@Second_Millennium.FemaleMan©_Meets_ OncoMouse™: Feminism and Technoscience*. New York: Routledge, 1997; Peter, J. Taylor et al. (eds), *Changing Life: Genomes, Ecologies, Bodies, Commodities*. Minneapolis, MN: University of Minnesota Press, 1997; Valerie Hartouni, *Cultural Conceptions: On Reproductive Technologies and the Remaking of Life*. Minneapolis, MN: University of Minnesota Press, 1997; Sarah Franklin and Helena Ragoné, *Reproducing Reproduction:*

Kinship, Power, and Technological Innovation. Philadelphia, PA: University of Pennsylvania Press, 1998; Paul Rabinow, *French DNA: Trouble In Purgatory.* Chicago, IL: University of Chicago Press, 1999; Adriana Petryna, *Life Exposed: Biological Citizens after Chernobyl.* Princeton, NJ: Princeton University Press, 2002; Alan Goodman et al. (eds), *Genetic Nature/Culture: Anthropology and Science Beyond the Two-Culture Divide.* Berkeley, CA: University of California Press, 2003; Sarah Franklin and Margaret Lock (eds), *Remaking Life and Death: Toward an Anthropology of the Biosciences.* Santa Fe, NM: SAR Press, 2003; Charis Thompson, *Making Parents: The Ontological Choreography of Reproductive Technologies.* Cambridge, MA: MIT Press, 2005; Susan Squier, *Liminal Lives: Imagining the Human at the Frontiers of Biomedicine.* Durham, NC: Duke University Press, 2005; Kaushik Sunder Rajan, *Biocapital: The Constitution of Postgenomic Life.* Durham, NC: Duke University Press, 2006; Nikolas Rose, *The Politics of Life Itself: Biomedicine, Power, and Subjectivity in the Twenty-First Century.* Princeton, NJ: Princeton University Press, 2006; Gisli Pálsson, *Anthropology and the New Genetics.* Cambridge: Cambridge University Press, 2007; Sandra Banford, *Biology Unmoored: Melanesian Reflections on Life and Biotechnology.* Berkeley, CA: University of California Press, 2007; Sarah Franklin, *Dolly Mixtures: The Remaking of Genealogy.* Durham, NC: Duke University Press, 2007; Mike Fortun, *Promising Genomics: Iceland and Decode Genetics in a World of Speculation.* Berkeley, CA: University of California Press, 2008; Melinda Cooper, *Life as Surplus: Biotechnology and Capitalism in the Neoliberal Era.* Seattle, WA: University of Washington Press, 2008; Lynn Morgan, *Icons of Life: A Cultural History of Human Embryos.* Berkeley, CA: University of California Press, 2009; Stefan Helmreich, *Alien Ocean: Anthropological Voyages in Microbial Seas.* Berkeley, CA: University of California Press, 2009; Niki Vermeulen et al. (eds), *Bio-Objects: Life in the 21st Century.* Farnham, Surrey: Ashgate, 2012; Keith Wailoo et al. (eds), *Genetics and the Unsettled Past: The Collision of DNA, Race, and History.* New Brunswick, NJ: Rutgers University Press, 2012; Kelly E. Happe, *The Material Gene: Gender, Race, and Heredity after the Human Genome Project.* New York: New York University Press, 2013; Kim TallBear, *Native American DNA: Tribal Belonging and the False Promise of Genetic Science.* Minneapolis, MN: University of Minnesota Press, 2013; Natasha Myers, *Rendering Life Molecular: Models, Modelers, and Excitable Matter.* Durham, NC: Duke University Press, 2015; Stefan Helmreich, *Sounding the Limits of Life: Essays in the Anthropology of Biology and Beyond.* Princeton, NJ: Princeton University Press, 2016; Alondra Nelson, *The Social Life of DNA: Race, Reparations, and Reconciliation After the Genome.* Boston, MA: Beacon Press, 2016; Sophia Roosth, *Synthetic: How Life Got Made.* Chicago, IL: University of Chicago Press, 2017.

11 See Sara Wylie, *Fractivism: Corporate Bodies and Chemical Bonds.* Durham, NC: Duke University Press, 2018.

Indigenous communities as well as immigrant, Black, queer, and trans peoples.[12] In the age of Covid-19, the matter of life came to be phrased in the urgent language of breath: of who might breathe when, where, and how, from the neighborhood to the polity to the climate-changing planet (think here of Black Lives Matter and its use of "I can't breathe," the dying words of the police-murdered Eric Garner and George Floyd, as a call to arms).[13] In the time of the pandemic, no one cared anymore about whether it might be possible to consider viruses on their own as alive; SARS-CoV-2 was entangled with life and life chances, common yet relentlessly unequal, at all scales.[14]

Through all of these moments, the pages of science journals have persistently asked and re-asked the question: "What is life?," in ways that have variously ignored, misrecognized—though, in rare cases, echoed—these more extended conversations. In the pages that follow, the reader will find an archive of the first pages of dozens of articles—and a few books—titled "What Is Life?," displaying what different authors, at different times, and in different scientific

---

[12] Michelle Murphy, "Alterlife and Decolonial Chemical Relations," *Cultural Anthropology*, vol. 32, no. 4 (2017), pp. 494–503. Mel Y. Chen, *Animacies: Biopolitics, Racial Mattering, and Queer Affect*. Durham, NC: Duke University Press, 2012. Kim TallBear, "Beyond the Life/Not Life Binary: A Feminist-Indigenous Reading of Cryopreservation, Interspecies Thinking and the New Materialisms," in Joanna Radin and Emma Kowal (eds), *Cryopolitics: Frozen Life in a Melting World*. Cambridge: MA: MIT Press, 2017; Cleo Assan Woelfle-Erskine, "The Watershed Body: Transgressing Frontiers in Riverine Sciences, Planning Stochastic Multispecies Worlds," *Catalyst*, vol. 3, no. 2 (2017), https://catalystjournal. org/index.php/catalyst/article/view/28840, accessed April 23, 2021; Max Liboiron, *Pollution Is Colonialism*. Durham, NC: Duke University Press, 2021.

[13] Marsha Rosengarten, "The Challenge of Breath: Toward an 'After' COVID-19," *Social Anthropology*, vol. 28, no. 2 (2020), pp. 342–43; and much more here: https://www.berghahnjournals.com/view/journals /aia/27/2/aia.27.issue-2.xml, accessed April 23, 2021.

[14] Soraya de Chadarevian and Roberta Raffaetà, "COVID-19: Rethinking the Nature of Viruses," *History and Philosophy of the Life Science*, vol. 43, no. 2 (2021), https://doi.org/10.1007/s40656-020-00361-8, accessed April 23, 2021. See also Natalia Zdorovtsova, "What Is Life? A Crash Course to Autopoiesis," *Varsity* (posted January 22, 2021), https://www .varsity.co.uk/science/20521, accessed April 23, 2021.

disciplines, from the late nineteenth century to today, have offered as possible paths toward answering that question.[15] Paging through these, it is as well to keep in mind something the historian of biology Evelyn Fox Keller once put succinctly:

> Questions elicit answers not only by the fact of being asked but by the form of their asking [...]. When does it make sense to ask a question of such a form, say, as—to take one conspicuous example—"What is Life?" What are the preconditions for the asking of such a question?"[16]

The following archive provides some data for asking about such preconditions, though also evidence for how the question, once posed, has set up parameters for a cascade of historically unfolding answers, calls and responses, attempts to make sense of why the question should be asked at all.

Interspersed with this archive are interruptions created by us, the Biogroop. We are four authors who, over the last decade or so, have met as a reading and writing collective in the anthropology and history of biology. Our offerings are genre-various works that do not so much try to respond to the "What is life?" question as spin off from it, surfacing unexpected or strange entailments of some of the ways the question has been posed and answered. There is no call for completeness here, no fidelity to one discipline's way of doing things, no demand for a new synthesis (though our sympathies as anthropologists and historians fall with those more recent demands to explode the category of "life" as any kind of essence). We hope our interventions as well as the archive itself generate further questions.

15 By working only with texts that carry the title "What Is Life?," inevitably we miss answers to the question that appear within differently titled pieces. In Ernest Everett Just, *The Biology of the Cell Surface* (Philadelphia, PA: P. Blakiston's Sons & Co., Inc., 1939), for example, the question is posed twice, with Just offering one answer as "Life is exquisitely a time-thing, like music" (p. 2).

16 Evelyn Fox Keller, notes on "life," possibly for Fall 1998 MIT Freshman Seminar STSA04: "What Is Life? A Historical Perspective on Law(s) and Order in Biology." From Evelyn Fox Keller's personal folder on "life" and its definitions, shared with the authors.

We think of the sequence of sample pages we have gathered as elements of the sort that the series editors of *Das Neue Alphabet* (DNA, The New Alphabet) seek to put into new combination, elements that, as they put it, can "function according to the principles of variation and permutation." Our own insertions into the sequence themselves press toward alternative ways of thinking, asking, or, perhaps, undoing the question: "What is life?"

Biogroop (Stefan Helmreich, Natasha Myers, Sophia Roosth, Michael Rossi)

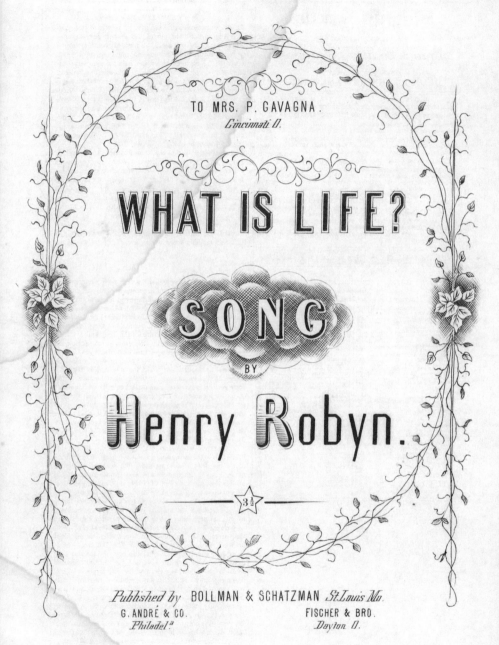

TO MRS. P. GAVAGNA.
Cincinnati O.

WHAT IS LIFE?

SONG

BY

Henry Robyn.

3½

Published by BOLLMAN & SCHATZMAN St. Louis Mo.
G. ANDRÉ & CO.   FISCHER & BRO.
Philadel.ᵃ   Dayton O.

272   **Scientific American.**   [MAY 4, 1878.

Scientific American.

ESTABLISHED 1845.

MUNN & CO., Editors and Proprietors.

PUBLISHED WEEKLY AT

NO. 37 PARK ROW, NEW YORK.

O. D. MUNN.   A. E. BEACH.

TERMS FOR THE SCIENTIFIC AMERICAN.

One copy, one year, postage included........................... **$3 20**
One copy, six months, postage included **1 60**

Clubs.—One extra copy of THE SCIENTIFIC AMERICAN will be supplied
gratis for every club of five subscribers at $3.20 each; additional copies at
same proportionate rate. Postage prepaid.

The Scientific American Supplement
is a distinct paper from the SCIENTIFIC AMERICAN. THE SUPPLEMENT
is issued weekly; every number contains 16 octavo pages, with handsome
cover, uniform in size with SCIENTIFIC AMERICAN. Terms of subscription
for SUPPLEMENT, $5.00 a year, postage paid, to subscribers.   Single copies
10 cents. Sold by all news dealers throughout the country.

Combined Rates.—The SCIENTIFIC AMERICAN and SUPPLEMENT
will be sent for one year, postage free, on receipt of seven dollars. Both
papers to one address or different addresses, as desired.

The safest way to remit is by draft, postal order, or registered letter.
Address MUNN & CO., 37 Park Row, N. Y.

☞ Subscriptions received and single copies of either paper sold by all
the news agents.

VOL. XXXVIII., No. 18. [NEW SERIES.] *Thirty-third Year.*

NEW YORK, SATURDAY, MAY 4, 1878.

Contents.

(Illustrated articles are marked with an asterisk.)

WHAT IS LIFE?

The best our dictionaries can give in answer to this question is the verbal definition of the French encyclopedia, "Life is the opposite of death," a form of words giving no clew to the nature of the phenomena, the aggregate of which we call life. Language has many pairs of similarly contrasted words, such as up and down, high and low, hot and cold, heavy and light; and to say that any one of these is not its opposite adds nothing to the definiteness of our conception of either. Are life and death, like the others we have cited, merely relative terms? Or is there such an entity as Life, the addition of which to not living matter makes it living; the subtraction of which from living matter makes it dead? Is life the result of organization, or is organization primarily the result of life? What *is* life?

When primitive man asleep in his hut dreamed of war and the chase, of journeying to distant places, conversing with the dead, and the like, his natural inference was that there was in him a special self which left the sleeping body at will, yet was forced to return on the waking of the body. And since he saw in dreamland the counterparts of everything he saw in waking life, he as naturally extended to all objects, dead as well as living, the double existence he imagined for himself.

Accordingly from the very dawn of history the conception of life as something supernatural, something superior to the bodily organization, which left the body temporarily in sleep and trance and the stupor of drunkenness or disease, and permanently on dying, has been familiar to all thinkers. The idea of life as the result or expression of material combination came much later. Later still came the compound theory of life held by Leibnitz and Descartes and their followers, who believed in a physical life for the body and a purely spiritual life for the mind. From this point of view the body is a machine, made up of mechanical devices and operated by mechanical or purely physical powers, while it is inhabited by a soul which thinks, but takes no part in the discharge of vital functions. In the words of Leibnitz, "The body goes on in its development mechanically, and the laws of mechanics are never transgressed in its natural motions; in the soul everything takes place as though there were no body, and in the body everything takes place as though there were no soul." This view makes life the product or expression of material combinations up to the point of consciousness; above that the soul is the life.

Of the three theories, the purely spiritualistic—that is, that life is due to the indwelling presence of spirit—is at once the oldest and still the most popular. This was the conception of Pythagoras, Plato, Aristotle, and Hippocrates. It has always been the theory of the Christian Church; and it underwent many vagaries at the hands of Christian mysteries, scholastics, alchemists, and other speculative writers during the Middle Ages. At one time it was believed that each and every vital process was the work of a particular spirit, and a man's comfort and character depended on the kind of spirits that pervaded and animated him. Such were the teachings of Basil, Valentin, Paracelsus, and Van Helmont. Stahl summarily dismissed all this infinite host of immaterial intelligent governing spirits save one, the rational immortal soul. In this view, which was the very principle of life. There had grown up in that day a school of chemist-doctors who resolved all the phenomena of life into chemical action. In opposition to those Stahl contended that the real life force was not only unlike the chemical force of ordinary matter, but that the two kinds of force were hostile to each other—life persisting only so long as the vital or soul force was dominant, death being the ultimate victory of the physical forces.

Stahl's immediate successors were soon compelled to reject the idea that vital force was an intelligent force; intelligence was relegated to the soul; but they retained the notion of antagonism between vitality and the laws of mechanics, physics, and chemistry. From this point of view Bichat de-

CONCEPTION EXPÉRIMENTALE DE LA VIE

I.

QU'EST-CE QUE LA VIE?

Le problème de la vie a été la question par excellence du philoso-phisme : chaque doctrine sur la vie a été la clef de voûte d'une école philosophique. La vie est le pivot autour duquel ont tourné les intelli-gences de tous les temps à la recherche obsédante de l'insaisissable mystère. Partout et en tout nous retrouvons dans le passé, nous reconnaissons dans le présent, nous entrevoyons dans l'avenir, cette même obsession du problème primordial de la *Loi de la Vie*. C'est que, en réalité, nous sentons implicitement, instinctivement, que tout ce qui intéresse notre pauvre humanité se rattache intimement et nécessaire-ment à la loi même de la vie. N'est-ce pas ce qui explique et ce qu'im-plique l'anthropomorphisme des premiers âges, d'où sont nées toutes les religions, et les religions n'empruntent-elles pas leur raison d'être et leur succès à la préoccupation par excellence de la vie, au problème de l'origine et de la destinée des êtres, absolument comme la médecine est née et a vécu du souci de la conservation de la vie? La philosophie ne se résume-t-elle pas en somme à la double conception spiritualiste et matérialiste de la vie? La civilisation n'est-elle pas le résultat de la recherche et de la conquête des moyens et des conditions de la vie? Nos rêves et nos aspirations, nos craintes et nos désirs, chantés par les poètes de tous les temps, sont-ils donc autre chose que l'expression de notre amour de tout ce qui tient à la vie? Le but suprême de l'art n'est-il pas de reproduire, de fixer, de perpétuer la sensation, l'illusion de la vie? La science, la recherche infatigable de l'inconnu, n'ont-elles donc pas toujours le même et unique but, la vie, soit pour en pénétrer les secrets, soit pour en faciliter les manifestations? La question sociale actuelle ne puise-t-elle pas sa force irrésistible aux sources mêmes de notre instinct de conservation?

WHAT IS LIFE?

By X. Y.

TORONTO:

THE COPP, CLARK COMPANY, LIMITED

1895.

WHAT IS LIFE ?   11

In all this there is nothing new or very strange ; the same vegetable does not grow in all temperatures, and there are many little growths of bodies, called animalculæ which move about in the water and receive their food in a way similar to the little snowflakes, for that

is what these little bodies are called as they float about in the air, or sink to the ground to die, like thousands of other little animals in the water. It may be said that it is the cold that makes the snowflakes grow, and that they will disappear in the heat ; quite true, but, is it not

WHAT IS LIFE?

A Discovery by Prof. Gates, of Washington, which Answers the Question.

An Interesting Subject.

" What is life?" This question has been asked during all ages, but it has never until now been successfully answered. Prof. Elmer Gates of Washington, who has been making great experiments with the microscope, has made virtually a double microscope; in other words, he brings the image of the first microscope on the lens, which picture on the lens is enlarged by the second microscope so that many things which it is impossible to see with an ordinary microscope are revealed. In this way he is able to see the smallest cells of the body in an exceedingly large form. He says: " Cut a piece of protoplasm into a number of pieces and each. piece will still be alive," thus proving that the germs of life exist in even the minutest particle of the body. But he goes farther and says that he believes mind is life, and that mind is present in every particle of the body. This is a new, a startling, a wonderful theory, and it may lead to a revolution on the subjects of disease, health, and of happiness. It explains clearly one thing and that is, why the mind is frequently affected when the body is disordered, and it brings home the question of health or disease very forcibly.

It becomes plain that in order to have a clear head and a strong mind one must have a body that is in perfect condition. When the body is deranged the mind cannot work rightly. With pains in the back, nausea, weariness, bearing down sensations, and all the symptoms indicating a weakened condition of the kidneys and urinary organs, there is certain to be a clouding of the intellect which calls for immediate action. This action can only be successfully taken by using some great, modern discovery that is certain to put the cell tissues in perfect shape. There is such a discovery and it is doing more to counteract pain and establish health than anything known to modern times. In speaking of it Dr. William Edward Robson of London says: " I emphatically state that I have been able to give more relief and effect more cures by the use of Warner's Safe Cure than by all the medicines in the British pharmacopœia." Doctor R. A. Gunn, dean of the United States Medical College, says: " I prescribe and use Warner's Safe Cure in both acute and chronic Bright's disease and commend it most frankly."

Such statements should convince any man or woman that there is no need of further suffering, if a prompt use is made of the remedy that is commended so highly.

German Warships Sail.

SINGAPORE, Straits Settlements, March 1.—The German warships Deutschland and Gefion under the command of Prince Henry, Prussia, sailed today for Hong Kong.

WHAT IS LIFE?

Evidence Toward Extra-Terrestrial Origin.

Mr. Herbert Spencer's definition of the nature of life implies, as is well known, a continuous adjustment of internal to external relations. In other words, vitality is preserved by interactions going on between the constituents of the protoplasm. On the face of it this view must be very materially modified in the light of some exceedingly interesting experiments recently brought to the notice of the Royal society by Mr. Horace Brown, whose classic researches on that interesting class of ferments the enzymes are well known. He has found that by submitting seeds to the very low temperature of evaporating liquid air—i. e., from 183 degrees C. to —192 degrees C.— for 110 consecutive hours, their power of germinating is not in any way impaired.

Since the above temperature is considerably below that at which ordinary chemical reactions take place the result is very remarkable and would appear to show that although a state of complete chemical inertness in protoplasm may be established it does not necessarily lead to a destruction of its potential activity. Is the protoplasm thus brought to a "resting" condition to burst into activity on restoring favorable conditions? If so, what becomes of life during the "rest?" These observations are also of interest in connection with the suggestion of Lord Kelvin that the origin of life as we know it may have been extraterrestrial and due to the "mossgrown fragments from the ruins of another world" which reached the earth as meteorites.

That such fragments might circulate in the intense cold of space for a perfectly indefinite period without prejudice to their freight of seeds or spores is, Mr. Horace Brown remarks, almost certain from the facts we know about the maintenance of life by "resting" protoplasm; the difficulties in the way of accepting such a hypothesis certainly do not lie in this direction. Here is an interesting problem for biologists, and the developments of the question will be followed with the keenest interest.—London Lancet.

WHAT IS LIFE?
OR
WHERE ARE WE
WHAT ARE WE
WHENCE DID WE COME
AND
WHITHER DO WE GO?

NOTICE.

THE war in South Africa has delayed the publication of the *Second* Edition of "What is Life?" This delay has enabled the author to revise his work "What is Heat?" and to add to it the consideration of the important fundamental problem, "What is Electricity?" Many new and very important fundamental experiments are described and explained, and a summary showing the actual natural reactions when gases are liquefied. The work is now published at the low price of 6s., by MESSRS. CHAPMAN & HALL, LTD. The title of the new edition is, "WHAT IS HEAT AND WHAT IS ELECTRICITY?"

LONDON, *November*, 1900.

FREDERICK HOVENDEN,

F.L.S., F.G.S., F.R.M.S.

WHAT IS LIFE?

the prime factor—the ETHER, through which the inherent properties of the atom or molecule are made active. Hence, no Ether, no regeneration.

10. The number of species of atoms is unknown, it is most likely an enormous number. We probably know about seventy of these species at present.

11. The fundamental factor in the formation of molecules, under the influence of Ether, is the selective and combining power of the strongest species of atoms.

12. From the combining power of the strongest species of atoms under the influence of Ether, arises the formation of cells.

13. Cells under the influence of the strongest cell group themselves to form highly complex structures or organisms, hence the most complex of all organisms —MAN. The activity of cells forms that activity we call Human Life. Thus Life is the sum of the activity or energy of molecules formed of atoms.

14. The power of the regeneration of molecules causes regeneration of cells, and this causes regeneration of Life. Life is eternal.

FREDERICK HOVENDEN

Here the facts actually known are duly set forth, and among other things it is shown that the rats were destroyed in great numbers, while it seems doubtful whether the 'ground-birds' were actually exterminated in any instance.

T. D. A. COCKERELL.

EAST LAS VEGAS, N. M.,
May 16, 1901.

AN EARTHWORK DISCOVERED IN MICHIGAN.

MR. G. N. HAUPTMAN, of Saginaw, Michigan, in a letter dated May, 1901, reports that 'there is on section 34, T. 21, N., R. 1 E., Ogemaw county, Mich., an earthwork [of horse-shoe shape]. The trench * * * is three feet' deep, and in it stand forest trees.

If any notice of this has ever been printed I should be glad to receive references to the same. I believe no note of this earthwork has previously been made, although four earthworks in the same county are well known and are recorded in the literature of archeology.

HARLAN I. SMITH.

PHYSIOLOGY IN THE SCHOOLS.

TO THE EDITOR OF SCIENCE: The writer has a 'horrible suspicion' that T. Hough imputes the physiological questions, to which he demurs, to him. He did not propound them. The high-school questions were taken from the text-book which the pupils had used, and if the text was legitimate, the questions were.

It is the writer's conviction that public school teachers are not generally qualified to teach physiology ; that physiology proper is too abstruse for the grammar grades ; and that the teacher in every grade should be expected to have a better knowledge of his subject than can be obtained from the elementary text placed in the hands of his pupils. Finally he may venture to express his fear that a little elementary knowledge of the reasons for the non-increase in stature of the human skeleton throughout life might not be amiss to his learned critic even.

S. W. WILLISTON.

SHORTER ARTICLES.

WHAT IS LIFE?

SOME thoughts, started by reading an article with the above title in *Nature*, Vol. 57, p. 138,

1898, by Horace Brown, and jotted down at that time, but laid aside, I have thought might perhaps interest the readers of SCIENCE, especially as the subject continues to be agitated.*

Heretofore in cases of dormant life, as in seeds kept for years, perhaps for centuries, or in dessicated infusoria, etc., in which under favorable conditions active life is revived, it has been supposed that very slow metabolic changes still go on during the state of dormancy—life is supposed to be feeble, but not extinct. The same was supposed to be the case in seeds or bacteria exposed to intense cold of $-180°$ to $-200°$ C. by Pictet or even $-250°$ by Dewar.

But it is now proved that at this temperature chemical affinity is destroyed and all chemical changes arrested, and therefore the chemical changes characteristic of life—metabolism—also must cease. But with the return of heat they revive. Therefore, in this case, life seems to spring spontaneously from dead matter. Must we then revive the old doctrine of spontaneous generation? If not we must change or greatly modify our conceptions of life.

From such experiments it is evident that, although life is, indeed, a distinct *form of energy*, yet its nearest alliance is with chemism. For as chemism is completely destroyed by extreme cold and again revived by heat, so life may be completely arrested by cold and again revived by heat—*if the molecular structure characteristic of living protoplasm* (whatever that may be) *remains unchanged.*

What then is the necessary condition of life— or, to put it clearly, what is the difference between *dead* protoplasm and *living* protoplasm, or rather protoplasm *capable of life?* Evidently it is not a difference in chemical composition, for no change in this regard takes place in the act of death. It is, I suppose, a difference in *molecular arrangement*—a difference in *allotropic condition.* As the necessary condition of chemical properties is a certain equivalent composition : so the necessary condition of vital properties is, in addition, a certain molecular constitution. But as equivalent composition may

Nature, Vol. 61, p. 67, 1899 ; Vol. 63, p. 420, 1901. *Revue Scientifique*, Vol. 15, p. 201, 1901, and SCIENCE, Vol. 12, p. 774, 1900.

What is Life?

By F. J. Allen, M.D. Cantab.,

Professor of Physiology in Mason University College.

Read before the Society, February 21st, 1899.

The question " What is Life " has probably presented itself to the minds of philosophers ever since philosophy began to exist. Various answers have been proposed, some of them purely fanciful, others having more or less reason. Among the more reasonable I may quote the following :

" *Aristotle* says ' Life is the assemblage of the operations of nutrition, growth, and destruction "; *Lamarck* states that ' Life, in the parts of the body possessing it, is that state which permits organic movements; and the movements which constitute active life result from the application of a stimulus'; *Bichat* says ' Life is the sum total of the functions which resist death '; *Treviranus* calls it ' The constant uniformity of phenomena, with diversity of external influences'; *Laurence* says 'It consists in the assemblage of all the functions or purposes of organized bodies, and in the general result of their exercise' ; *Duges* calls it ' The special activity of organized bodies'; *Béclards' definition is 'Organization in action';* *   *   *   *

These theories are quoted as collated by Professor M'Kendrick :* I will add certain others which are discussed by Mr. Herbert Spencer in his *Principles of Biology.*†

Schelling said that Life is the tendency to individuation. *Richerand* gives the definition, " Life is a collection of phenomena which succeed each other during a limited time in an organized body." * * * * " Life," according to De Blainville, is the twofold internal movement of composition and decomposition, at once general and continuous." * * * * Mr. G. H. Lewes suggests the definition " Life is a series of definite and successive changes, both of structure and composition, which take place within an individual without destroying its identity."

To these Herbert Spencer adds three definitions of his own : the

---

* " Text Book of Physiology," 1888, Vol. I, p. 31.

† Edition 1864, Vol. I, chap. IV.

THE AMERICAN
JOURNAL OF PSYCHOLOGY

Founded by G. STANLEY HALL, in 1887.

| VOL. XIV. | JANUARY, 1903. | No. 1. |

WHAT IS LIFE?

LECTURE DELIVERED AT CLARK UNIVERSITY.

By JUSTUS GAULE,

Professor of Physiology, University of Zurich.

Not many years since tradition would have had a ready answer to this question. The whole Middle Ages is characterized by the tradition that life is a process caused in the body by the soul, or, in other words, by a living power. It was something supernatural that caused life, something eluding investigation, not subordinate to the laws of nature. In the meantime, mankind has been forced from this attitude toward the problem of life by necessity,—necessity, that is, the sufferings of mankind and the desire to heal or, at least to ameliorate them. Out of this sympathy and the wish to heal disease medical science has arisen. It first began by collecting facts concerning everything known that would alleviate pain, but, in proportion as this store of experience grew, in proportion as the attempt was made to systematize this knowledge, in other words in proportion as the art of healing began to be taught as a science, it was no longer possible to ignore the fact that disease is a change in the processes of life, and that it was only possible to recognize the changes when it was known what had been changed, that is, what life is. Thus, Physiology, the study of life, came to form the foundation of medical science. This Physiology has already developed some conceptions of life as a scientifically recognizable process. It is in these conceptions of life that I wish to introduce certain modifications and it is of these that I wish to speak to you to-day. My modifications are dictated by the apprehension that the now prevalent ideas concerning the phenomena of life

WHAT IS LIFE?

BY SIR OLIVER LODGE, PRINCIPAL OF THE UNIVERSITY OF
BIRMINGHAM.

PRELIMINARY REMARKS ON RECENT VIEWS IN CHEMISTRY.

IN a recent article, Sir William Ramsay wrote on the question,
"What is an Element?" and incidentally remarked the fact that
the groupings possible to atoms of carbon are exceptionally
numerous and complicated, each carbon atom having the power
of linking itself with others to an extraordinary extent, so that
it is no exceptional thing to find a substance which contains
twenty or thirty atoms of carbon, as well as other elements, linked
together in its molecule in a perfectly definite way; the molecule
being still classifiable as that of a definite chemical compound.
But there are also some non-elementary bodies which, although
they are chemically complete and satisfied, retain a considerable
vestige of power to link their molecules together so as to make
a complex and massive compound molecule; and these are able
not only to link similar molecules into a more or less indefinite
chain, but to unite and include the saturated molecules of many
other substances also into the unwieldy aggregate.

Of the non-elementary bodies possessing this property, *water*
appears to be one of the chief; for there is evidence to show that
the ordinary H_2O molecule of water, although it may be properly
spoken of as a saturated or satisfied compound, seldom exists in
the simple isolated shape depicted by the above formula, but
rather that a great number of such simple molecules attach themselves to each other by what is called their residual or outstanding
affinity, and build themselves up into a complex aggregate.

The doctrine of residual affinity has been long advocated by
Armstrong; and the present writer has recently shown that it is
a necessary consequence of the electrical theory of chemical

Examines Frozen Monkey

THE MONKEY
AND THE
TARDIGRADE

Dr. C. C. Warn, general manager of the Los Angeles Humane Department, examining a frozen monkey, preparatory to an experiment by Dr. Ralph Willard in revivification. Dr. Willard is observing the physician's examination.

I've been through contretemps," said the old tardigrade,
"I've been frozen and poisoned and fried,
Dessicated, hypoxied, and shot into space,
And yet for all that I've not died."

Tardigrades, also known as "water bears" or "moss piglets" or "bear animalcula," are microscopic, multicellular creatures known for their ability to suspend metabolic processes under conditions of extreme environmental stress. In this suspended state, tardigrades can endure otherwise lethal levels of, for example, radiation, heat, cold, pressure, and toxic chemicals. Thus, as one commentator put it, they remain "apparently dead for a long time, reviving again when wetted." Arnold Lang, *Text-book of Comparative Anatomy*. New York: Macmillan and Company, 1891, p. 545. For a recent, popular view, see Cornelia Dean, "The Tardigrade: Practically Invisible, Indestructible 'Water Bears.'"

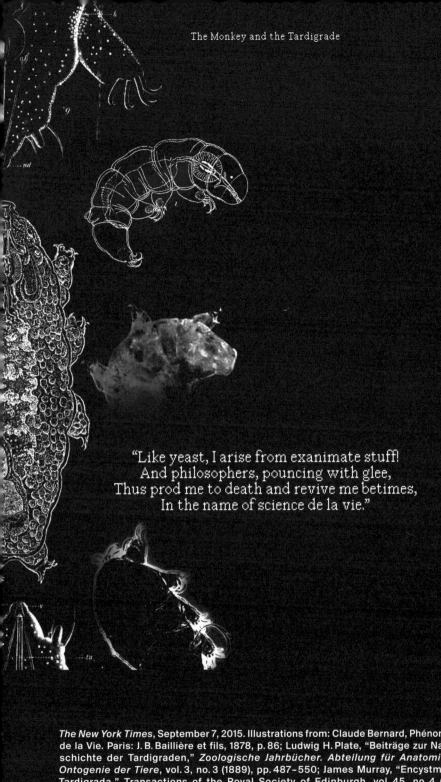

"Like yeast, I arise from exanimate stuff!
And philosophers, pouncing with glee,
Thus prod me to death and revive me betimes,
In the name of science de la vie."

The New York Times, September 7, 2015. Illustrations from: Claude Bernard, Phénomènes de la Vie. Paris: J. B. Baillière et fils, 1878, p. 86; Ludwig H. Plate, "Beiträge zur Naturge-schichte der Tardigraden," *Zoologische Jahrbücher. Abteilung für Anatomie und Ontogenie der Tiere*, vol. 3, no. 3 (1889), pp. 487–550; James Murray, "Encystment of Tardigrada," Transactions of the Royal Society of Edinburgh, vol. 45, no. 4 (1908), pp. 837–54; Janice M. Glime, "Tardigrade Survival," in *Bryophyte Ecology*, volume II [ebook]. Houghton, MI: Michigan Technological University, n.d., chapter 5, subsection 6, www.bryoecol.mtu.edu, accessed April 1, 2021.

"Such is my lot: mortal coils? But a farce
(more precisely, called 'cryptobiosis'),
Where meaningful contrasts 'twixt lively and croaked
Seem silly and vain, if not bogus."

"But then what, I must ask, is this 'science of life'?
What truth does it claim to expose?
For a hundred (plus) years, I've heard sounded the call:
'What is life?' And still nobody knows."

"What does life look like? What does life weigh?
Is life hard, rough, or smooth? Is it slimy?
It's a dubious premise, on which to base science;
Has a project seemed ever less likely?"

"Oh, I'm beginning to think that life doesn't abide
In the ways that it's typically taken —
As a thing in the world, ontologically true
It seems catagoric-mistaken."

"And with all this in mind; I gloomily mull:
Is life real? Is it true? Or just junk?
Thus I ply the beyond; I am doomed to persist
in a deep metaphysical funk."

Claude Bernard was among the first commentators to think about the ability of tardigrades to suspend and resume metabolic activity as a pertinent aspect of the question of the nature of life processes in general. In his 1878 *Phénomènes de la Vie*, he listed the tardigrade as an exemplar of "latent life"—life that was not-quite life, not just yet—likening their rejuvenative ability to that of seeds. Somewhat less than a century later, biologist David Keilin used the term "cryptobiosis" to describe this state of not-death but not-life, writing that cryptobiosis was "the state of an organism when it shows no visible signs of life and when its metabolic activity becomes hardly measurable, or comes reversibly to a stand-still" (David Keilin, "The Problem of Anabiosis or Latent Life: History and Current Concept," *Proceedings of the Royal Society of London*, vol. 150 (1959), pp. 149–91). Whether latent life, abiosis, cryptobiosis, or some as-yet-uncoined term, tardigrades' particularly durable structural integrity has made them a leading candidate for inquiry into both the limits and origins of life, including the Panspermia hypothesis: the notion that life on Earth might have extraterrestrial origins. This in turn has involved exposing tardigrades to space-like conditions, such as vacuum, high levels of radiation, hypoxia, and freezing temperatures, in order to see whether a cryptobiotic state might enable an organism to survive the stresses of a deep-space voyage and reentry into a planet's atmosphere.

"Ahoy hoy!" called a monkey, drifting by in a suit,
Please forgive my sudden ape-earance.
But I happened to hear your distressed colloquy
And thought I'd supply you coherence."

Tardigrades are not the only creature to inspire flights of fancy about the reversibility and irreversibility of life processes. During the early 1930s, one Dr. Ralph Willard, a research chemist living in Hollywood, California, indulged in what can only be described as a five-year bender of reanimation—freezing and attempting to revive hundreds of small animals, including frogs, guinea pigs, and—ultimately—two tubercular rhesus monkeys named Jekal and Matilda. Matilda never came to after being frozen, but Jekal did. He emerged from his state of suspended animation, said Dr. Willard, foul-tempered but lively, and showing no signs of his former tuberculosis. It is worth noting here that Willard's purpose was apparently more therapeutic than resurrectory. He seems to have been far more impressed by the idea that freezing killed tuberculosis than by the idea of bringing monkeys back to life, evidently envisioning a sort of cryotherapy in contrast to chemotherapy. Encouraged by his success with Jekal, Willard next set out to freeze and reanimate a human being—specifically, a muscular, young screenwriter named Steven Simkhovich. The scheme, however, ran afoul of the law, which evidently frowns upon freezing and reviving humans, and Willard was forced to cease his experiments.

> "(For a 'Hollywood doctor' once froze me to death
> In August, 1935,
> And I stayed in that state for almost a week
> Until, Tardigrade-like, I revived)."

See: "Frozen Pig," the *Milwaukee Journal*, May 15, 1935; "Monkey Restored to Life After Five-Day 'Death,'" *Reading Eagle*, August 1935; "Monkey Revived After Being Frozen Stiff," *Sarasota Herald-Tribune*, August 6, 1935; "Frozen Monkeys," the *New York Times*, August 8, 1935; "Man Agrees to Become 'Human Icicle' in Test," the *Evening Independent*, August 10, 1935; "Human Icicle Step Pondered: Chemist May Drop Plan or Move to New York for Test," the *Miami News*, August 13, 1935; "Law May Halt Freezing Plan of Physician," *Sarasota Herald-Tribune*, August 13, 1935.

"And my frozen sojourn left me in no doubt:
Life is there, for the sketching and seeing!
If the abstracted notion of life seems unreal
Can you distrust the Great Chain of Being?"

"See here, my small friend! It can plainly be seen
With the help of my visual aids,
That life is a union of traits that bind creatures
From great whales to low tardigrades."

Fig. 253. The sizes of organisms.

Tardigrades and monkeys are not alone among experimental animals, though each, in their own way, demarcates a particular episteme in thinking about the order of living things. For example, to Galen—the second-century Greek physician whose anatomical studies informed a millennium of European academic medicine—vivisection of apes and monkeys provided a suitable substitute for human bodies which, for reasons both legal and customary, could not be vivisected or dissected. In this, Galen was interested principally in tracing the functioning of particular organs, especially arteries and veins. The analogy he drew between apes and humans was primarily functional, though also affective. He evidently left most of the work of vivisection to his slaves, preferring not to witness first-hand the agony of his experimental subjects. For Claude Bernard and his ideological descendents today, on the other hand, the relationship between tardigrades and humans was and is one of an abstract sense of life and life processes. What one can learn from freezing and irradiating tardigrades is more informative of the general notion of life-as-a-subject-of-biology and less of any particular anatomical or functional specificity. The cladistic representation of life as trees, meanwhile, entwines in complicated ways these parallel notions of anatomy and physiology, on the one hand, and life itself, on the other.

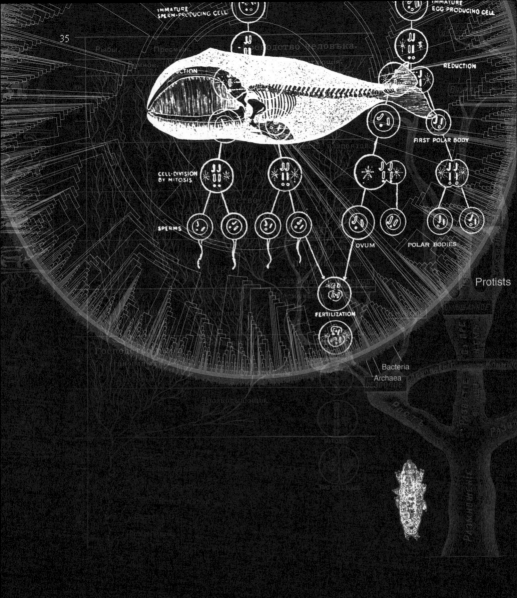

Protists

Bacteria
Archaea

"Some winged, some leafy, some spongy, some bald,
Some earless or ear'd on their knees,
But all can respire, reproduce, and evolve,
And what's more can be noted on trees!"

For a straightforward visual history of cladograms, see Theodore W. Pietsch, *Trees of Life: A Visual History of Evolution*. Baltimore: Johns Hopkins University Press, 2012. See also Ian Hacking, "Trees of Logic, Trees of Porphyry," in J. Heilbron (ed.), *Advancements Of Learning: Essays in Honour of Paolo Rossi*. Florence: Olshki, 2007, pp. 146–97. Illustrations from: H. G. Wells, *The Science of Life*. London: Cassels, 1929 ("The Size of Organisms," p. 937; "Evolution of the Placental Mammals during the Cenozoic Period," p. 778; "A Summary in Diagram Form of how the Chromosome Outfit is Handed from one Generation to the Next," p. 464; "A Vestigal Leg," p. 364); David Hillis, "Circular cladogram," *Science*, vol. 300, no. 5626 (2003), pp. 1692–97; and "Tree of Relations," in V. V. Lunkevich, *Ostovy Zhizny*, 1910, p. 109.

"Furthermore…" he went on, but the microbe said "Stop!
These are all living things, that is true,
And arranged in a way that makes them make sense
But is 'life' just 'what-living-things-do'"?

"No, that's too rotund — definition sans tooth.
(Is 'sleep' just 'the state of a sleeper?')
To commune with the deepest-most Benthian truths
We must venture a little bit deeper."

Envisioning life as a "chain" or a "tree" of being is simply one level of abstraction. In a more concrete mode, consider the representation of life through metaphors of mechanical and chemical processes. One thinks here, for instance, of chemical diagrams which stand synecdochally for living things themselves. One thinks also of life as interpreted through life-like shapes and forms: crystals, for instance, or crochet patterns, or self-reproducing reactions which generate the shapes of living things, like mushrooms. And one likewise thinks of life as confirmed through the metaphor of artifice: cellular machines, molecular machines, biostatistical measuring devices, and so forth. See, for example, Sophia Roosth, *Synthetic: How Life Got Made*. Chicago, IL: The University of Chicago Press, 2017.

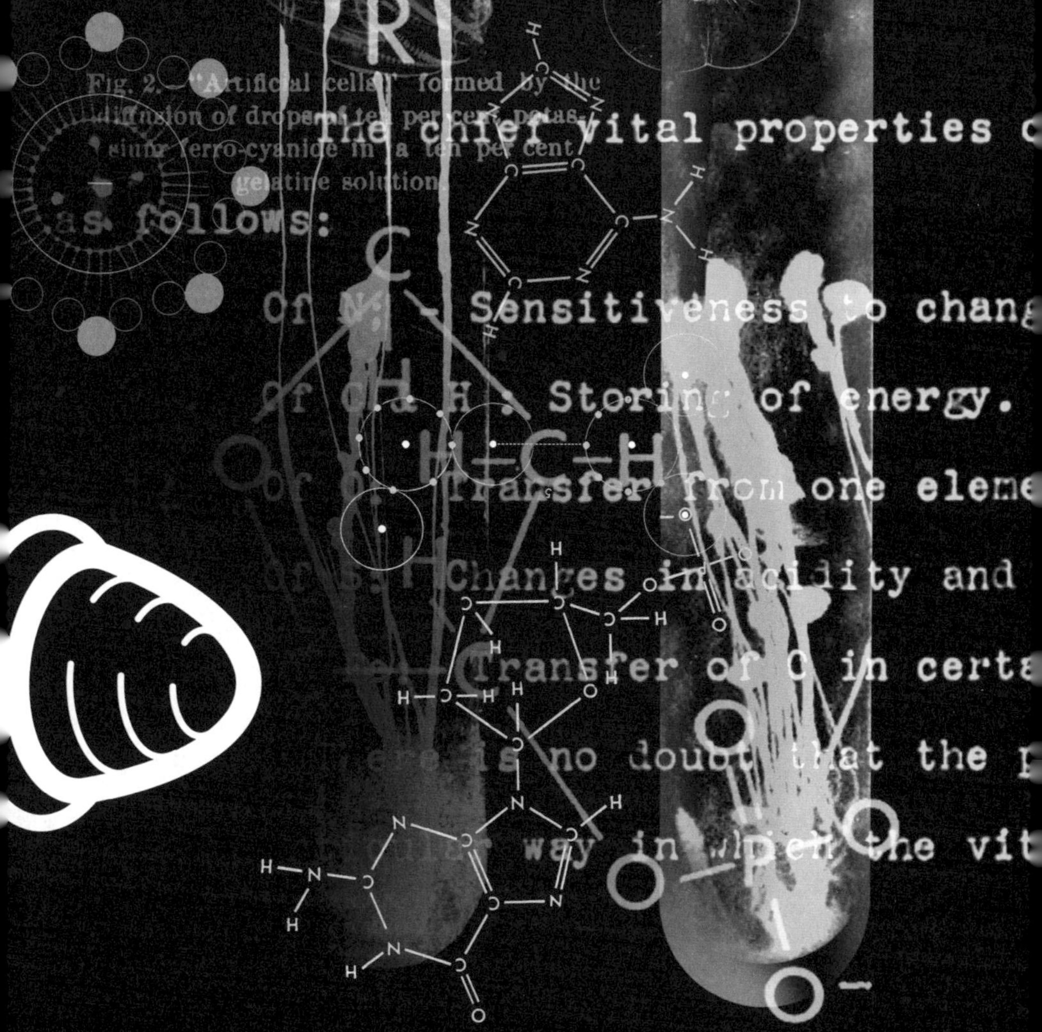

Fig. 2. "Artificial cells" formed by the
diffusion of drops of ten per cent potassium ferro-cyanide in a ten per cent
gelatine solution.

The chief vital properties

as follows:

Sensitiveness to chang

Storing of energy.

Transfer from one eleme

Changes in acidity and

Transfer of C in certa

There is no doubt that the

similar way in which the vit

"Ah, erm," said the monkey, "perhaps I misspoke."
"The trees need not be so central.
Just imagine instead, life drawn out to expose
Its building blocks most elemental!"

Illustrations from: Benjamin C. Gruenberg, "The Creation of Artificial Life: The Making of Living Matter from Non-Living," *Scientific American*, vol. 105, no. 11 (1911), pp. 231–37 ("An Artificial Plant Which Was Produced in a Test Tube" and "Artificial Organs Showing Mushroom Shape," p. 231); F. J. Allen, *What Is Life?* Birmingham Natural History and Philosophical Society, 1899, p. 9; George Wald, "The Origins of Life," *Scientific American*, vol. 191, no. 92 (1954), pp. 44–53; and Otto Larink and Wildried Westheide, *Coastal Plankton: Photo Guide for European Seas*. Munich: F. Pfeil, 2006 ("Plankton," pp. 37, 39, 45, 51, 55, 63).

Illustrations from: Francis Gano Benedict and Edward Provan Cathcart, *Muscular Work: A Metabolic Study with Special Reference to the Efficiency of the Human Body as a Machine*. Washington, DC: Carnegie Institution of Washington, 1913 ("Bicycle Ergometer and Universal Respiration Apparatus," frontispiece); Fritz Kahn, "Der Mensch als Industriepalast," 1926; A. Gibor (ed), *Conditions for Life: Readings from Scientific American*, San Francisco: W. H. Freeman, 1976 (Richard J. Wurtman, "Some Direct and Indirect Effects of Light," p. 127 and "Chlorophyll Molecule," p. 300); Paul Doty, "Proteins," *Scientific American*, vol. 197, no. 3 (1957), pp. 173–87 ("Random Chain," p. 176); from Emile Zuckerkandl, "The Evolution of Hemoglobin," in R. Haynes and P Hanawalt (eds), *The Molecular Basis of Life: An Introduction to Molecular Biology*. San Fransisco, CA: W. H. Freeman, 1968 ("Family Resemblances are Exhibited by Polypeptide Chains," pp. 317–18); and Trudy McKee and James R. McKee, *Biochemistry: The Molecular Basis of Life*. New York: Oxford University Press ("In Aerobic Cells Most Energy Is Generated Within the Mitochondrion," p. 272)

BLC

"Yes Yes! Here it is! Life at its most base!
Think: 'atomic continuous motion,'
Molecules struggle; protoplasm
Takes shape — life is order in seas of commotion."

"Here nitrogen, oxygen, carbon and more
Combine to form organelles!
Which synthesize proteins and make energy
In the tiny machines we call 'cells.'"

"And species and genus and orders and such
Come together to form life's cartels
Then consciousness dawns! The cosmos unites!
(To paraphrase Herbert George Wells)."*

"Through these ingredients, science reveals
The hum of a finite sublime:
Life is matter and heat — electricity,
Too — all subtending the primal urschleim!"

*If I may adventure to interject: That is a slightly overwrought paraphrase. What I said, in fact, was: "we have seen the interdependence of individuals in space increase with the development of colonial and gregarious forms and of individuals in time with the growing care and intimacy of parent for the young. The higher forms of interdependence have involved great extensions of mental correlation. [...] This mental modification is steadily in the direction of the subordination of egotism and the suppression of extremes of uncorrelated individual activity. [...] We have already, if this account of mental processes is sound, the gradual appearance of what we may call synthetic super-minds in the species Homo sapiens, into which individual consciousnesses tend to merge themselves. [...] At the end of our vista of the progressive mental development of mankind stands the promise of Man, consciously controlling his own destinies and the destinies of all life upon this planet."—H.G. Wells, *The Science of Life*. Glasgow: The Waverly Publishing Co., 1931, pp. 1474–75.

But before the monkey could continue his thought
His discussant jumped in without shyness:
"You've given a picture of life, that is true,
But it's a picture of life rendered lifeless!"

"In chemicals, atoms, and physical forces
Is the concept of life not forsaken?
If that's all there is, then I'll find my peace
In spontaneous regeneration!"

Further consider the idea of life abstracted as information processes. Foregoing a vital-
istic complexity in favor of the algorithmic, this can be best represented, for example, as
life in silico rather than in vivo. See, for example, Martin Gardner, "Mathematical Games:
The Fantastic Combinations of John Conway's New Solitaire Game 'Life,'" *Scientific
American*, vol. 223, no. 4 (1970), pp. 120–23. The particular form opposite was developed
by R. W. Gosper, also in 1970. See also Stefan Helmreich, *Silicon Second Nature: Culturing
Artificial Life in a Digital World*. Berkeley, CA: University of California Press, 1998.

"Fine! Fine!" cried the ape, "Once more to the breach!
Don't get yourself into a snit!
Let's diagram life as a system dynamic
Of accretions of order, to wit."

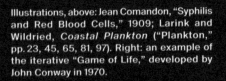

Illustrations, above: Jean Comandon, "Syphilis
and Red Blood Cells," 1909; Larink and
Wildried, *Coastal Plankton* ("Plankton,"
pp. 23, 45, 65, 81, 97). Right: an example of
the iterative "Game of Life," developed by
John Conway in 1970.

"Think of life as a pattern, a structure, a code!
Underlying all things organismic
Whether wetware or soft-; anaerobic or airy,
All life is, at base, algorithmic!"

"Information arrays! Feedback and flows!
Networks and nets — and what's better:
Our friend, DNA, reminding us all, that
Life is a word (with four letters)!"

And this vision of life-as-mathematic-sublime
Seemed to him to be simply, profusely
So profound, up and down, that he bounded around
And danced the informatic watusi.

It is worth pointing out here that the watusi—as a successor to the twist—stands in a long line of entwined, helical dances; if these do not echo, precisely, the helical structure imparted to the "molecule of life" by contemporaneous science, the watusi nevertheless conveys something of its sinuous vitality. Of course, as Marshall Kramer points out, one must also consider the mashed potato, then, as a precursor to its own sort of vital dance, echoing not only the mashed ferments of Louis Pasteur's lab, but also the mashed precursors to PCR, which amplifies the utility of DNA.

Illustrations from: Èdouard Monod-Herzen, *Principes de Morphologie Générale*. Paris: Gauthier-Villars, 1957, pp. 14, 18, 60; Robert Ransom, *Computers and Embryos: Models in Developmental Biology*. Chichester and New York: J. Wiley, 1981, pp. 40, 116, 122, 151.

Then the simian paused, and looked down with a sigh
"But I suppose you'll reject all that, too.
"Matter and trees; structure and code
"Is there anything more I can do?"

"There, there," said the microbe, a touch of concern
On his face (though it was miniscule);
"There's no need to be blue — you've done quite a lot.
'Can it be, life just won't follow rules?"

"Why, all of these atoms and patterns and such
"That you set out before my small eyeses
"Have helped me see life as historical chance
'Upon which one philosophizes."

"Could it be that life's both more and less
"Than one thing? Could it be that 'life' really comprises
"Relations and signs, risky and thick? That
"Ontologically, life is surprises?"

"Duration and flesh, noise and sensation!"
"Atoms too?" Asked the ape.
"Sure! Why not?"
"Entangled with bios and zōē? That's great!
"We'll throw it all into the pot!"

Then excited they grew,
their heads in a blur,
And they agreed to do more life-work soon.
But first, hand in hand,
upon life's remand,
They danced by the lively moon, the moon.

They danced by the lively moon.

¿ QUE ES LA VIDA ?

POR

LUIS RAZETTI

Vice - Rector de la Universidad Central de Venezuela.
Secretario perpetuo de la Academia de Medicina.
Profesor de Anatomia humana.

IMPRENTA NACIONAL

— 1907 —

XXX

DEFINICION DE LA VIDA

—

De acuerdo con los hechos demostrado por la experimentación científica en el campo de la química biológica y según los principios de la Filosofía monista, que establece la ley de la unidad del Universo infinito y eterno, podemos formular la siguiente definición de la vida:

LA VIDA ES UN PROCESO FÍSICO-QUÍMICO QUE SE VERIFICA EN LA MOLÉCULA VIVIENTE, COMO RESULTADO DE LAS LEYES GENERALES DE LA MATERIA, Y EN EL CUAL NO HAY INTERVENCIÓN, NI REMOTA, NI ACTUAL, DE NINGUNA FUERZA Ó PRINCIPIO DISTINTO DE LA ENERGÍA.

—

LA VIDA PSÍQUICA, INTELECTUAL Y MORAL DEL HOMBRE, ES EL RESULTADO DE LA ACTIVIDAD FUNCIONAL DE LAS CÉLULAS NERVIOSAS DE LA CORTEZA CEREBRAL, QUE COMO TODAS LAS CÉLULAS VIVAS, OBEDECEN Á LAS LEYES GENERALES DE LA MATERIA ORGANIZADA, ES DECIR, QUE EN SU FUNCIONAMIENTO NO INTERVIENE NINGÚN PRINCIPIO SUPERIOR É INMATERIAL.

sleepwalk

triable

𝔚𝔥𝔞𝔱 𝔦𝔰 𝔏𝔦𝔣𝔢?

Published in 1908 by
PETER F. SWING

Many words are found in dictionaries which show attributes of life. Of these, the word energy seems the most appropriate. That which is alive becomes dead when it ceases to have motion, or when all energy is gone and it is still. What is energy? Power, force, motion. How many forces or powers are there in the universe—one or many? And, if many, what are they? It is my belief there is but one energy, or force, in the universe, and from the nature of things there can be but one. Why more than one? If more than one, might they not come in conflict?

We see manifestations of force on all sides—the winds, the tides, flowing water, steam, the explosion of gases, earthquakes, vulcanism, the pressure of the air, gravitation, living beings, the lifting of water out of the ocean and its return to the earth, the expansion of substances, beasts, fowls, fishes and growing vegetation.

Let us analyze these so-called forces and see whether they are true forces, possessing power of action, or whether they are resultants or manifestations of other forces.

Take the power of the winds. Is that an independent energy? The wind is simply air put in motion by some

EXPOSITORY ESSAYS IN CHRISTIAN
PHILOSOPHY
Edited by the Rev. FRANCIS AVELING, D.D.

WHAT IS LIFE?

A STUDY OF

VITALISM AND NEO-VITALISM

BY

BERTRAM C. A. WINDLE
M.A., M.D., SC.D., LL.D., F.R.S., F.S.A.
PRESIDENT OF QUEEN'S COLLEGE, CORK

Pulchra quæ videntur, pulchriora quæ existimantur, longe
pulcherrima quæ ignorantur

LONDON AND EDINBURGH
SANDS AND COMPANY
ST. LOUIS, MO.
B. HERDER, 17 South Broadway
1908

28   WHAT IS LIFE

body and then drawing the remainder up to the promontory which has been put forth. Thus it is able to move itself from place to place. But beyond this we may observe the granules which generally exist in the protoplasm to be also in movement.

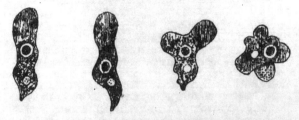

Amœba, showing clear ectoplasm, granular endoplasm, dark nucleus, and lighter contractile vacuole   *(From Verworn.)*

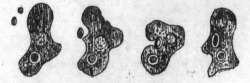

Amoeba devouring a plant cell; four successive stages of ingestion. (From Verworn)

Fig. II.

We can see that these "stream constantly forwards along the central axis of each process as it forms, and backwards within the clear layer all round, like a fountain playing in a bell-jar."[1]

So that the movements take place within the creature and it is also able to transport itself from

[1] Hartog.

WHAT IS PHYSICAL LIFE
ITS ORIGIN AND NATURE

BY

WILLIAM HANNA THOMSON, M.D., LL.D.

Author of "Brain and Personality"

CONSULTING PHYSICIAN TO THE ROOSEVELT HOS-
PITAL; TO THE NEW YORK STATE MANHATTAN
HOSPITALS FOR THE INSANE; AND TO THE NEW
YORK RED CROSS HOSPITAL; FORMERLY PROFESSOR
OF THE PRACTICE OF MEDICINE AND OF
DISEASES OF THE NERVOUS SYSTEM, NEW YORK
UNIVERSITY MEDICAL COLLEGE; EX-PRESIDENT
OF THE NEW YORK ACADEMY OF MEDICINE, ETC.

NEW YORK
DODD, MEAD AND COMPANY
1909

WHAT IS LIFE ON MARS LIKE?

BY EDMUND FERRIER

THAT most Olympian of astronomers, Le Verrier, at a sitting of the French Academy of Sciences, once cast at his critics this scornful phrase: "Sit down, gentlemen. I will express myself in terms that can be understood even by botanists." And not once, but many times, has the modest science of plants and flowers with as much ease and self-confidence been relegated to the furthermost extreme from the giddy speculations as to the origin of worlds that astronomy deals in. But the discussion which is proceeding on the subject of the canals of Mars is calculated to humble the pride of the learned gentlemen who suppose themselves to have made a final conquest of the heavens. The appearance of Mars during the nights of December, 1911, when it burned so brightly in the sky, distinguishing itself clearly among the stars by its yellow color, and the eloquence with which the American astronomer, Professor Lowell, defends his theory as to the canals, have made the question of what is going on on the surface of that planet a subject of important controversy.

The history of the observations is a singular one. In 1877 the Italian astronomer, Schiaparelli, announced that he had discovered on the surface of the planet a network of dark, straight lines which bound together across the continents a number of seas and which could only be immense canals constructed by intelligent beings. Almost at the same time the astronomers Burton and Dreyer, without knowing anything of Schiaparelli's observations, reported a similar discovery. Such a coincidence left scarcely any doubt as to the reality of the facts. Schiaparelli pursued his observations with vigor; a number of astronomers — Christie, Proctor, Lowell, Douglas, Pickering, Flammarion, and others—set themselves to examine Mars continuously. Sec-

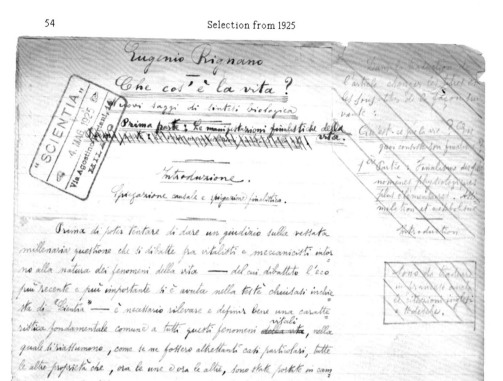

Eugenio Rignano

Che cos'è la vita ?

Nuovi saggi di sintesi biologica

Prima parte: Le manifestazioni finalistiche della vita.

Introduzione.

Spiegazione causale e spiegazione finalistica.

Prima di poter tentare di dare un giudizio sulla vessata millenaria questione che si dibatte fra vitalisti e meccanicisti intorno alla natura dei fenomeni della vita — del cui dibattito l'eco più recente e più importante ti è avuta nella testè chiusa inchiesta di "Scientia" — è necessario rilevare e definire bene una caratteristica fondamentale comune a tutti questi fenomeni vitali, nella quale si riattumono, come se ne fossero altrettanti casi particolari, tutte le altre proprietà che, ora le une ora le altre, sono state poste in campo come caratteristiche appunto dei fenomeni vitali stessi. E questa loro caratteristica fondamentale è quella dell'aspetto finalistico o teleologico, che tutti i fenomeni della vita presentano nelle loro manifestazioni più tipiche.

Non è certo facile definire in che consista il finalismo, o, sia pure, l'apparenza finalistica di un dato fenomeno. Bisogna all'uopo partirsi, inevitabilmente, dall'uomo, misura di tutte le cose. L'uomo spiega le azioni coscienti e volontarie dei propri simili comparandole alle proprie, e siccome per introspezione egli osserva che gli atti da lui compiuti lo sono per soddisfare dati bisogni o desideri, cioè per raggiungere dati scopi o fini, così egli attribuisce scopi e fini analoghi agli atti dei propri simili, e con tale ipotesi perviene a « spiegare » la condotta di questi ultimi, nel modo per lui pragmaticamente più utile.

Per i suoi bisogni, i suoi scopi, i suoi fini, l'uomo anche inventa e costruisce la più grande varietà di artefatti — case, prodotti di ogni genere, macchine per ottenere questi prodotti, ecc. — adatti a soddisfare o a raggiungere questi bisogni, questi scopi, questi fini. Ciascuno di questi

82   SCIENTIFIC AMERICAN   FEBRUARY, 1926

Dr. MacDougal and (on the left) Dr. Clarke, the author, trying to duplicate the elusive life process with the artificial cell

What Is Life?

The Puzzling Phenomenon Called "Life" Is Being Studied by Means of a Working Model of a Living Plant Cell

By Beverly L. Clarke

WE are so far from a perfect understanding of life that even active workers in biological research cannot agree as to the real nature of life—whether it is purely a matter of chemistry and physics and evolution and chance, or whether there will indeed prove to be an element of the nature of the "spark of life" of the ancients, transcending mortal understanding.

Of great interest in this connection are some recent experiments by a distinguished American physiologist, Dr. D. T. MacDougal, Director of the Carnegie Institution of Washington's Laboratories for Plant Physiology at Tucson, Arizona, and Carmel, California.

For many years Dr. MacDougal has been studying the phenomenon of life by a very rational method. He has chosen as his materials chemical substances of the same nature as those occurring in living matter, and has subjected them, singly and in combinations, to the various conditions to which living material itself is normally exposed. He has made elaborate studies of the action on these materials of certain physical processes believed to play important roles in life.

Such a process is that known as swelling, wherein certain semi-solid substances like gelatin, when immersed in water, will attract to themselves molecules of water which they hold with great force, with consequent increase in size. There is no doubt that swelling is an intimate associate of most life processes. Someone has suggested that the mechanism of muscle action is simply a matter of swelling and shrinkage of the muscle fibres. Dr. MacDougal has invented an instrument (shown on page 83) for making an automatic record of the swelling in liquids of gelatin plates or of sections cut from the living cactus plant.

It is now generally known that the unit of living matter is the cell. The cell is the building-stone—the brick—from which all plants and animals are

constructed. Life may indeed be regarded as the resultant action of the cells of which the organism is composed. What more natural, then, than to concentrate attention on the single cell? There is little doubt that these microscopic objects hold the key to the full understanding of life.

Dr. MacDougal has made a deep study of the known facts about cells. He has dealt particularly with plant cells, but that does not destroy the general character of his results. Viewed as a piece of architecture—as one would view a large building or the ground-plan of a town—the cell is a fairly simple affair. Figure 1 gives a general idea of the plant cell. It develops from a tiny mass of jelly, and the first change is perhaps a matter of self-protection—the outer layer of this ball of jelly undergoes a hardening process which forms it into a tough protecting sheath.

Most Primitive Plants Are Single Cells

As the cell enlarges, first by the addition of more material and then by absorption of water, the central portion becomes a hollow, water-filled cavity and the jelly-like protoplasm is pushed towards the outer wall to form the soft, semi-solid layer we call the plasma, or plasmatic layer. If now we place in the plasmatic layer a number of dark-colored bodies, the picture is complete. The simplest plants and animals—the ancestors of us all—consist of only one cell which under the microscope looks very much like this.

The natural sequel to Dr. MacDougal's series of researches on the chemistry of protoplasm was an attempt to construct a model of the living cell, of similar materials arranged in similar relations to each other as in the actual cell.

Much experimentation was necessary before the present model of the "artificial cell" was designed. Figure 2 shows this model. The framework on which the cell is built is a paper thimble about one inch in diameter and three inches high. This thimble,

being pure cellulose, also serves admirably as the external cell-wall.

The first step in the limitation of the plant cell is the deposition within the meshwork of which the cellulose thimble consists, of substances of jelly-like composition and jelly-like consistency. Such substances are agar-agar, which is extracted from a kind of sea-weed and comes in crisp flakes like breakfast food, and pectin, a similar material found abundantly in apples. These substances are dissolved in boiling water to a thick, brownish syrup, into which the thimble is dipped. In order to obtain the desired physical structure, the thimble is now treated with alcohol, which abstracts part of the water. Next is prepared a solution of a mixture of gelatin and agar in proper proportions. To this is added a small quantity of some fat, a little soap, and a minute trace of salt. All these are included to represent actual conditions in plant protoplasm, which contains a very small amount of a great many substances. A layer of this hot mixture, a quarter of an inch thick, is applied to the inner surface of the thimble and allowed to harden, representing the plasmatic layer.

A rubber stopper carrying glass tubes is inserted in the thimble, and a solution of sugar is poured in to represent the cell sap. The "artificial cell" is now ready for operation.

What will it do? In general, it may be answered that this artificial cell will do a great many things that its living model does. If the cell, constructed as described and filled with sugar solution, is placed in a glass beaker containing either pure water or a solution of some salt, water alone or water plus particles of salt will pass through the cell wall and into the solution of sugar. If the cell was originally full of sugar solution, any further liquid passing into it will cause an overflow through the tube B (Figure 2), the amount of which overflow serves as a measure of the activity of the cell.

In the case of the living cell, much is known about

WHAT IS LIFE?
WHERE IS IT? HOW IS IT MANIFEST?
WHAT DOES IT SIGNIFY?

By

WILLIAM PATTEN

We cannot find life in any one time, or place. It has no one where, nor one beginning, nor is it interrupted like the ticking of a clock. We lose its beauty and its significance when we pick it to pieces, because the "all-together" action we call life is not in separate cells, nor in protoplasmic particles, nor yet in their environments, any more than the beauty and significance of a cathedral is in its bricks and mortar, or in the resources of its native country, or in all the priests and artists, kings and peasants, that have helped to make it what it is. Life is everywhere and everlasting. It is manifest in the work of all things, all times, and all places, just as they are.

* * *

A natural phenomenon is a creative act that shows us how Nature carries on Her creative business and what She creates. It speaks to us saying: Behold! Here am I. Learn of me.

The whole complex of Nature-action is a larger kind of metabolism; and metabolism, like "business," is but another name for all the inner and outer activities of life. In the cosmic organism that we call Nature, there are no inactive parts, nor empty places. Every part has its own creative value, and plays its part in its own way, in its own time and place, in coöperation with its fellows. All the so-called "living things," and the so-called "dead," are fellow workers, fellow actors and reactors, fellow givers and receivers, creators and destroyers, in this universal life of Nature.

In that larger kingdom, as in the plant and animal kingdoms, every part works and is created by work. Life *is* creative work. It is the work of give and take between the big workers here and the little work-

1

WHAT IS LIFE?

BY

AUGUSTA GASKELL

INTRODUCTION

By Karl T. Compton
Professor of Physics, Princeton University

By Raymond Pearl
Professor of Biology, The Johns Hopkins University

CHARLES C THOMAS

SPRINGFIELD, ILLINOIS - BALTIMORE, MARYLAND

1928

RC

Peculiarity of the organism.—Unique qualities not found in non-living matter.

8. *Peculiarity of the dual-system.*—Unique dynamics.

Peculiarity of the organism.—The same.

9. *Peculiarity of the dual-system.*—The end of the process is a separate happening for every indidivual dual-system.

Peculiarity of the organism.—Death is an individual happening for every organism.

10. *Peculiarity of the dual-system.*—After the separation of the Z-system from the Y-system (the atoms and molecules of the Y-system no longer being bound together by the interlocking of the Z-system, and only chemical bonds remaining) the Y-system collapses.

Peculiarity of the organism.—After death the body disintegrates.

11. *Peculiarity of the dual-system.*—Marked peculiarities of molecular formation (of the substances of the Y-system), because the uniting of atoms into molecules takes place as a (chemical) process that is secondary to the activities of the Z-system.

Peculiarity of the organism.—The marked peculiarities of organic substances. (*See* p. 92.)
E. J. Holmyard says: "While the general laws of chemistry apply to organic substances and

Life — JUST A KICK IN THE slats
Schopenhauer Zilch

you said it

Stefan Helmreich
Life and the Compass

When Inspector Treviranus, of the Buenos Aires police, retrieved the tattered, calf-bound genealogy book from his grandmother's abandoned mansion in San Telmo, he found himself puzzled by an annotation next to the name of Ludolph Christian Treviranus, that German ancestor of his about whom he'd heard, now and again, such strange and perplexing tales.

Ludolph Christian, who had lived from 1779 to 1864, had conducted experiments, unorthodox, even in his own time, in animal magnetism. Adherents of animal magnetism held that a magnetic fluid suffused living things and might be enticed to flow between bodies (through the air, as a kind of pseudo-sublimate), permitting the relay of physical influence across organisms not otherwise touching.[1] That much, the Inspector already knew. His grandmother had told him all about *mesmerism* (as this enterprise eventually came to be known, after the German physician Franz Mesmer), when she had given him the gift of a magnetic compass, those many years ago, for his tenth birthday.

But the annotation reawakened in him a recollection of something far stranger—that Ludolph Christian had believed, not only, as so many advocates of the theory of animal magnetism had, in the projection of magnetic energy across space (permitting a woman in London, for example, to be "magnetized" by a doctor in Berlin, if only

---

1 Robert Darnton, *Mesmerism and the End of the Enlightenment in France.* Cambridge, MA: Harvard University Press, 1968; Geoffrey Sutton, "Electric Medicine and Mesmerism," *Isis*, vol. 72, no. 3 (1981), pp. 375–92; Adam Crabtree, *From Mesmer to Freud: Magnetic Sleep and the Roots of Psychological Healing.* New Haven, CT: Yale University Press, 1993; Alison Winter, *Mesmerized: Powers of Mind in Victorian Britain.* Chicago, IL: University of Chicago Press, 1998; Jonathan Miller, "Going Unconscious," in Robert Silvers (ed.), *Hidden Histories of Science.* New York: New York Review of Books, 1995, pp. 1–35; F. Scott Scribner, *Matters of Spirit: J. G. Fichte and the Technological Imagination.* University Park, PA: Penn State University Press, 2010.

that medic had a lock of her hair[2]) but believed, also, that magnetic energies might transport living intensities across time, might even permit organisms long departed—this would include people—to rematerialize later in history. The annotation, rendered in his grand-mother's arthritic hand, read, simply: "Treviranus appears, August 18, 2014, 34° 58' S, 58° 39' W."

Had his grandmother believed that, in just two days, some apparition of Ludolph Christian would be magically, magnetically, projected into the cemetery in the neighborhood of Recoleta, the location pinpointed by the coordinates? Though Ludolph Christian was not buried in Recoleta (his body was far away, indeed, in Bonn), the Inspector's grandmother would have been well within her usual habits to entertain such an eccentric conviction. It would be of a piece with her lifelong fascination with the *magnetobiology* of Alexander Chizhevsky, an early twentieth-century Russian biologist who had held that Earth's geomagnetic field could be modulated by magnetic storms on the sun, with formative effects on creatures ranging from the bacterial to the plant to the animal.[3] Chizhevsky, controversially, had even held that "revolutions and social catastrophes are influenced

2   Anon, "Magic, Witchcraft, and Animal Magnetism," *The Journal of Psycho-logical Medicine and Mental Pathology*, vol. 5. London: John Churchill, 1852, pp. 292–322, 297. The Romantic poet Samuel Taylor Coleridge wrote in the marginalia of one of the books of his library—this according to and quoted in Henry Nelson Coleridge (ed.), *Specimens of the Table Talk of the Late Samuel Taylor Coleridge*. London: Harper & Brothers, 1835, pp. 87–88—"Nine years has the subject of Zoo-magnetism been before me. I have traced it historically, collected a mass of documents in French, German, Italian, and the Latinists of the sixteenth century, have never neglected an opportunity of questioning eye-witnesses, e.g. Tieck, Treviranus, De Prait, Meyer, and others of literary or medical celebrity, and I remain where I was, and where the first perusal of Klug's works had left me, without having moved an inch backward or forward. The reply of Treviranus, the famous botanist, to me, when he was in London, is worth recording: 'Ich habe gesehen was (ich weiss das) ich nicht würde geglaubt haben aus *ihrer* erzählung,' &c. 'I have seen what I am certain I would not have believed on *your* telling; and in all reason, therefore, I can neither expect nor wish that you should believe in mine.'"

3   Alexander Chizhevsky, Земное эхо солнечных бурь (The Terrestrial Echo of Solar Storms). Moscow: Mysl, 1976 (first published in 1936).

by solar activity."[4] In the last few years, the Inspector's grandmother had started extending such thinking to the spirit world, and had taken to delivering nightly monologues about dead souls wandering the realm of invisible energies, seeking out and whispering confidences to the living. On nights when she was convinced that it was possible to sense the magnetic magnitudes of the dead, she would look up from her evening yogurt, gaze just past the Inspector's shoulder and say, cryptically, "Get out your compass. Everything points to it."

The Inspector had never been one to hold with such metaphysical, mystical ideas. That is why he had become a detective, after all; it was a profession he took to be all about transmuting the mysterious into the empirical. The compass his grandmother had given him had become a symbol for him of his commitment to objectivity, to measured reason, to science—not a pointer to the preternatural. Not something to use to find ghosts, not something to employ in scouting out... Ludolph Christian. He had never understood why his family had not paid more attention to the accomplishments of Ludolph Christian's elder brother, Gottfried Reinhold (1776–1837), who had worked in a far more sober area of inquiry and, indeed, had been a key figure in naming the science of living things, to which he had given a designation that stuck: *Biologie*, the term that titled his 1802 book. The Inspector preferred *that* family forebear, not the one who had sought to reunite three-legged cats, through "magnetism," with their lost limbs (though the stories about cats always gave him a pang, recalling to him the cat he'd had at age eleven; it had died from eating magnetic fingerprint powder with which Treviranus had been experimenting during some juvenile efforts at sleuthing).

Rationalist that he was and wanted to be, there was nonetheless something about the inscription that drew the Inspector into a reverie, into daydreaming about encountering a ghostly Ludolph Christian wandering through Recoleta, perhaps canvassing the attitudes of flowering plants, which he had investigated, during his life, with the eye of a Romantic philosopher, trained as he was by the Naturphilosoph Friedrich Wilhelm Joseph von Schelling. The Inspector

---

4 Mikhail N. Zhadin, "Review of Russian Literature on Biological Action of DC and Low-Frequency AC Magnetic Fields," *Bioelectromagnetics*, vol. 22, no. 2 (2001), pp. 27–45.

from time to time had himself, as a kind of mental exercise, taken up puzzles in the philosophy of biology. He found it galvanizing to ponder biological phenomena, for they struck him as not quite logical, though simultaneously as processes that might yield to explanation if only approached with appropriate definitions and precision. He wondered what Ludolph Christian would have said had he lived to see the discrediting of his theories of animal magnetism. Would work like Darwin's, full of mechanistic forces, have swept away his beliefs in shadowy magnetic energies?

As it happened, the Inspector had lately had Darwin on his mind, having returned a few days previous from walking the Camino de Darwin, a trail tracing Darwin's passages through Uruguay in the 1830s during his *Beagle* days (the Inspector had packed his compass and had been able to connect many of the dots on his own with a copy of Darwin's journal in hand). He'd grimaced that the bureaucrats in Montevideo had named the trail the Camino de Darwin, as though it were a path of religious pilgrimage. The Inspector's own attachment to Darwin as a figure of disenchantment had, to be sure, something of the pious to it, even if he would have been reluctant to admit that—though it had manifested quite sharply in his sense of the heresy of Darwin Desbocatti, the Uruguayan radio personality whose embarrassment of a book, *Yo, Darwin* (found in even the most upscale bookstores in Montevideo) promised not a theory of the origin of species, but rather *a theory of irreversible circular misfortune* ("teoría de la desgracia circular irreversible").

But the inscription: the appointment?—sometime this week?— with... *was* it meant to be with Ludolph Christian? How much better it would be if—crazy thought—it were Gottfried Reinhold! He'd have so much to talk about with this more reasonable brother... though even Gottfried Reinhold had experimented with animal magnetism, writing in volume 5 of his *Biologie* of an experiment he had conducted to "magnetize" a young woman, an experiment that had gone unexpectedly wrong when she fell into an eight-day sleepwalk.[5] Under most circumstances, the Inspector, rationalist that he was, would have dismissed his grandmother's scribble and its insane implication, but, stirred by a sense that he had left things unresolved, unsettled, with her, he kept paging through the book. Looking at the fading name of one ancestral figure after another, he noticed, here and there, pasted-in clippings, selections of academic articles it looked like, which all seemed to be in one way or another about unsolved questions in biology.

His grandmother had sometimes added scarlet circles and underscores to the article extracts. Maybe these were some kind of extended cryptogram or commentary, a key to what the inscription *really* meant. His own sometime interest in the life sciences had emerged under his grandmother's oblique tutelage, as he sought to explain away, to dismiss, her various assertions about life and magnetism. She had talked in bizarre ways about her own approaching death for ages, how she believed that life never ended, that it just moved from one state of matter, one manifestation, to another. "But you're too dedicated to common sense to believe that," she had scolded him.

5   Gottfried Reinhold Treviranus wrote:
     "[T]he influence of certain touches by human beings on other human beings
     has already been long observed. Mesmer seems to have been the first
     to discover that this influence is expressed most exquisitely when the indi-
     vidual being magnetized is stroked from the brain toward the peripheral
     ends of the nerves by the individual who is doing the manipulation. The
     stroking is more effective than mere touching. In cases where the recep-
     tivity for animal magnetism is very great, however, the mere laying on of
     hands, or even of close cohabitation, produces all the appearances of
     somnambulism with certain persons. I have had a case in which a seven-
     teen–year-old girl who, otherwise healthy and strong, in the initiating
     period was suddenly stricken with convulsions, and gradually fell into
     somnambulism, which in its greatest extent continued eight days without
     interruption, despite that I had attempted no more than a mere stroke
     with the flat hand at the beginning of the illness, and also this only a few
     times. Somnambulism is, however, seldom an effect of magnetism.
     Usually only fever follows, whereby evacuation is again set up, which was
     suppressed before, especially in the monthly purge."
     Gottfried Reinhold Treviranus, *Biologie: oder Philosophie der lebenden
     Natur für Naturforscher und Aerzt*, vol. 5. Göttingen: J. F. Röwer, 1818, p. 391.
     Translation by Joan Steigerwald, communicated to Stefan Helmreich,
     January 16, 2015.

"Even if you're at my side when I die, you won't believe what your compass will be sure to tell you—that things are reorienting."

The first piece he came across had been carefully excerpted from a 1905 number of the *North American Review*. In "What Is Life?" the author, Oliver Lodge, had written:

> Life may be something not only ultra-terrestrial, but also even immaterial, something outside our present categories of matter and energy; as real as they are, but different, and utilizing them for its own purpose.[6]

That strange anti-materialist claim sounded like one his grandmother might have endorsed.

The next piece had been clipped from a medical journal and, at first reading, seemed to offer a view similar to Lodge's. Written by an Antonio García Valcárcel and published in a 1952 issue of *Medicina española*, it was from a piece entitled "¿Qué es la vida?." Treviranus' eyes alighted on a passage around which his grandmother's hand had drawn a shaky oval:

> Is there any essential difference between those we designate as living beings and those we term inorganics or inanimate?
> For my part, I am inclined to reject that thesis. This implies a fundamental change in our concept of life.[7]

At least this pronouncement refused to jettison the material world. But: *no essential difference* between living beings and the inorganic or inanimate? Why had his grandmother encircled that passage? It sounded very much at odds with what he knew Treviranus—actually both Treviranus brothers—had believed; they had held that *viable* or

---

6 Oliver Lodge, "What Is Life?," *The North American Review*, vol. 180, no. 582 (1905), pp. 661–69.

7 "¿Existe alguna diferencia esencial entre los que designamos como seres vivos y los que calificamos de inorgánicos o 'inanimados'? Por me parte, come ya dejé sentado en artículos anteriores, me incline a una respuesta negativa. Ello implica un cambio fundamental en nuestro concepto de vida." See Antonio García Valcárcel, "Mecánica clásica y mecánica biológica; qué es la vida?," *Medicina española*, vol. 28, no. 165 (1952), pp. 485–96, here p. 486.

tratus.

palpable matter—"matter capable of life" (*lebensfähige Materie*)—was distinct from other sorts of stuff.[8] They maintained that organic, living matter was animated by a life force, which they called the *Lebenskraft* (life-craft), which would emerge into *life* with the aid of a formative force, the *Bildungskraft*, which was responsible for shaping the organism.[9] The *Lebenskraft* might *employ* forces of electricity and magnetism—which would be operative both inside and outside the organism—but the *Lebenskraft* itself was not reducible to these or to any other forces (as Treviranus had put it, "the actual secret of living nature will not be disclosed")[10]. (One historian of biology, he knew, had summarized Treviranus' thinking this way: "death does not involve a transition to lifeless matter, but instead through viable matter is a transformation into other forms of life.")[11] The argument in "¿Que es la vida?"—that there was nothing essentially vital *in* the organic—was, perhaps, one that his grandmother could, paradoxically, fuse with its opposite, permitting her to believe simultaneously in the endurance of life across substrates *and* in the inessentiality of any particular material.

Was his grandmother's gathering these quotations together her attempt to find some way to read scientific texts, however tendentiously, to give credence to her beliefs that people and their dispositions could travel through time, could move from animate to inanimate, material to immaterial, and back again? Did *that* have anything to do with "Treviranus appears, August 18, 2014, 34° 58' S, 58° 39' W"?

He found a 1902 comparison of "life" to a kite:

The kite is ever falling, but ever being lifted by the energy of the wind: so the Nitrogen of the living substance is ever falling

8   Joan Steigerwald, "Treviranus' Biology: Generation, Degeneration, and the Boundaries of Life," in Susanne Lettow (ed.), *Reproduction, Race, and Gender in Philosophy and the Early Life Sciences*. New York: State University of New York Press, 2014, pp.105–27.

9   Andrea Gambarotto, "Vital Forces and Organization: Philosophy of Nature and Biology in Karl Friedrich Kielmeyer," *Studies in History and Philosophy of Biological and Biomedical Sciences*, vol.48, part A (2014), pp.12–20, here p.18.

10 Quoted from ibid., p.18.

11 Steigerwald, "Treviranus' Biology," p.113.

into an inert state and being lost, only to be substituted by a fresh supply of active Nitrogen from the surrounding nutrient substances.[12]

This was also about renewal, regeneration. And he knew—because his grandmother had never tired of mentioning it—that wind was animated by energy from the sun, and that the sun could intervene, sometimes dramatically, in Earth's magnetic field, interventions that the Russian magnetobiologist Chizhevsky had made the cornerstone of his work (which he also sometimes called *heliobiology*, because of the centrality of the sun). Chizhevsky's was a magnetism that affected, shaped, *life* at all scales—a relatively modern refinement and expansion, the Inspector mused, of notions of animal magnetism, which had postulated that the magnetic fluid coursing through the body and, possibly, across bodies, was forced into motion by larger scale phenomena, such as tides.[13] Tides were processes, he knew, that many animals could sense. He'd read somewhere about dogs being able to predict the rise and fall of the sea.

In her final years, the Inspector's grandmother had come to be fascinated by the Buenos Aires dog walkers: people who could hold up to twenty dogs on their leashes at a time, captaining fleets of canines across busy streets. She had always noticed, she said, when a particular dog vanished from its usual cohort—and she wondered whether the other dogs could communicate somehow with their lost compatriots, perhaps even across the mortal threshold (whenever he heard this question, he pushed away any thoughts about his departed cat). Maybe his grandmother had had thoughts like these about humans, too. It wouldn't be surprising; after the dirty war of the late 1970s, when tens of thousands of Argentines had disappeared under the state terror, those left behind wondered whether they would ever again hear the voices of their lost ones. What was life that it could vanish, but somehow never leave?

---

12 F. J. Allen, "What is Life?," *Birmingham Natural History and Philosophical Society*, vol. 11 (1902), pp. 44-67, here pp. 54-55.
13 Simon Schaffer, "The Astrological Roots of Mesmerism," *Studies in History and Philosophy of Biological and Biomedical Sciences*, vol. 41, no. 3 (2010), pp. 158-68.

A loosely glued snippet fell out, from Lynn Margulis and Dorion Sagan's 1995 book, *What Is Life?*. It contained a picture of a magnetic bacterium:

Magnetotactic bacterium remnant with internal magnetosomes[14]

Here was animal magnetism—microbial magnetism?—again, though radically transformed. If nineteenth-century animal magnetism's fluid had been shown definitively to be imaginary, magnetism had not fully severed its possible connection to life, and to its ebb and flow from one place to another. Margulis and Sagan reported in their book on *magnetosensitive* organisms, creatures tuned to Earth's magnetic field, capable of aligning themselves according to the points of the compass—or at least to magnetic North and South.[15] Such microbes hosted *magnetosomes*, organelles that kept creatures oriented with respect not just to their local environment, but also to the larger scale of the planet Earth itself. Biologists postulated that these biogenic magnets permitted organisms to navigate chemical gradients, to locate zones of optimal chemical concentration in three-dimensional space. Here was life entwined with the magnetic. And death, too: cells

14 Lynn Margulis and Dorion Sagan, *What Is Life?*. Berkeley, CA: University of California Press, 1995, p. 220.
15 See also Richard B. Frankel and Richard P. Blakemore, "Magnetite and Magnetotaxis in Microorganisms," *Bioelectromagnetics*, vol. 10, no. 3 (1989), pp. 223–37.

were known to align magnetically even after life.[16] These organisms were compasses.

The outlandish claims of the animal magnetists—that living things might be suspended in fields of large-scale flows—seemed, after a fashion, to be true. Even the seventeenth-century Scottish physician William Maxwell's *De medicina magnetica* seemed to be prefiguring later, more sensible, accounts of the suffusing force of the magnetic: "There is a universal attraction, or what some people call a world-soul, it is life, as fire and ethereal as light itself. All matter would be destitute of action, except when this life-force, magnetic force, permeates it."[17] And, according to the latest biology, of course, not only microbes were geomagnetically attuned; bees, many birds, and some fish also hosted biogenic ferromagnets that helped them get around local landscapes and even (for birds) hemisphere-long stretches of space.[18] "What is life?" Answer: a phenomenon situated in the gradient flow of the world, which includes the magnetic field of the Earth.

The Inspector's thoughts kept circling around like this, traveling now and then toward tangents that seemed promisingly, potentially relevant. He noticed that he was nervously toying with his old compass, which seemed now not to be a talisman of objectivity, but a thoroughly Earth-bound artifact, tuned to the local, not the universal. If life on Earth, he asked himself, were modulated in particular ways by geomagnetism, wouldn't that unfold differently on other planets? That seemed the implication of another "What Is Life?" piece he

16 David B. Dusenbery, *Life at Small Scale: The Behavior of Microbes.* New York: Scientific American Library, 1996.

17 William Maxwell, *De medicina magnetica libri III. In quibus tam Theoria quam Praxis continetur; Opus Novum, admirabile et utilissimum ubi multa Naturae secretissima miracula panduntur spiritus vitalis operations....* Frankfurt, Johann Peter Zubrodt, 1679. The Inspector's grandmother had this book, too. She had also taken to reading the works of Athanasius Kircher, and liked to repeat his dismissal of animal magnetism—"there is but one magnet in the universe, and from it proceeds the magnetization of everything existing"—though seemed to be recuperating it into her own, idiosyncratic, magnetorheology.

18 Joseph L. Kirschvink, "Magnetite Biomineralization and Geomagnetic Sensitivity in Higher Animals: An Update and Recommendations for Future Study," *Bioelectromagnetics*, vol. 10, no. 3 (1989), pp. 239-59.

found in the genealogy book, this one from 2004 by Chris McKay, an astrobiologist at NASA. McKay's text spotlighted a meteorite found in Antarctica, which had arrived on Earth thirteen thousand years ago, having been blasted off Mars sixteen million years previous by the impact of another meteorite. Inside this putatively Martian rock were elliptical shapes that some scientists believed to be outlines of ancient microbial life. The one possibly organic material left behind in this extraterrestrial sample was magnetite. McKay underscored the significance of the substance: "Microbes don't readily form convincing fossils; the one exception may be the strings of magnetite formed by magnetotactic bacteria."[19] Here, the magnetic was a sign of life, a signature, something that could secure the presence of an entity through a telling absence. These dead Martians might be magnets.

(He thought, again, of his cat. He'd buried it in a patch of grass next to his grandmother's house, telling himself its death was not his fault, not really; it didn't help that, for weeks afterwards, his compass kept pointing him back to its grave.)

His thoughts returned to the cemetery, and to the annotation.

Was the Inspector's grandmother's annotation itself something like the magnetic organelles of the magnetotactic microbes he'd just read about, a device made to point to some important destination? Or was Treviranus making this whole thing up, as his late colleague, the metaphysical detective Erik Lönnrot, had turned out to be doing when tracking a baroque mystery a few years back? In an episode dramatic enough to qualify as material for a made-for-TV movie, Lönnrot had surmised that a pattern of murders might be unfolding across the city according to a numerological logic—points on the compass, as it happened—a pattern that, it turned out, materialized *only when Lönnrot named and started following it* (and announced to an interested newspaper reporter that he was doing so...), inspiring the very murderer that he and the Inspector were pursuing to execute Lönnrot's predicted path of homicides, ending in the death of Lönnrot himself.

Maybe definitions of life were like that: magnets that attracted data, which confirmed scientists' favorite definitions. Maybe such

19 Chris P. McKay, "What Is Life—and How Do We Search for It in Other Worlds?," *PLoS Biology*, vol. 2, no. 9 (2004), e302.

definitions were even circular.[20] Biologist Douglas E. Dix, in "What Is Life? Prerequisites for a Definition of Life," in the pages of the *Yale Journal of Biology and Medicine*, seemed to think so: "since we cannot define animate matter except in contrast to inanimate matter, we are in danger of circular reasoning: animate matter is what manifests life and life is what is manifested by animate matter."[21] Or maybe definitions of life were spiral, pointing outward to new definitions. That image might well describe the activities of those synthetic biologists who had lately created magnetic yeast.[22] If living things had not previously been magnetic, new science would make them so. Life was always being made anew by those people who sought to investigate it. The category of life was a philosophical, technical, and historical chimera, much like the field of biology itself, "a pastiche, a conglomeration of different methods and tools and points of view and approaches."[23]

This was too much. Treviranus had to get some air. He left the house. He took the genealogy book with him, though not without a certain nervousness. By anxious instinct, he took out his compass,

20 Certainly, the figure of the circle—or of circular, self-reinforcing processes —sometimes appeared at the center of discussions of the definition of life. One of the more storied examples was the theory of autopoiesis, which argued that organisms were continually engaged in the processes that permitted them to operate as unitary wholes. See Francisco J. Varela, et al., "Autopoiesis: The Organization of Living Systems, Its Characterization and a Model," *Biosystems*, vol. 5, no. 1 (1987), pp. 187-96; see also Sergey Tsokolov, "A Theory of Circular Organization and Negative Feedback: Defining Life in a Cybernetic Context," *Astrobiology*, vol. 10, no. 10 (2010), pp. 1031-42.

21 Douglas E. Dix, "What Is Life? Prerequisites for a Definition of Life," *Yale Journal of Biology and Medicine*, vol. 75, nos 5-6 (2002), pp. 313-21, here p. 317.

22 Keiji Nishida and Pamela Silver, "Induction of Biogenic Magnetization and Redox Control by a Component of the Target of Rapamycin Complex 1 Signaling Pathway," *PLoS Biology*, vol. 10, no. 2 (published February 28, 2012), doi.org/10.1371/journal.pbio.1001269.

23 Oren Harman and Michael R. Dietrich, "Introduction: Outsiders as Innovators in the Life Sciences," in Oren Harman and Michael R. Dietrich (eds), *Outsider Scientists: Routes to Innovation in Biology*. Chicago, IL: University of Chicago Press, 2013, pp. 1-23, here p. 21.

and, for good measure, his iPhone GPS. He found himself approaching the Recoleta cemetery. Ambling among the open-air cafés lining the Plaza Francia and sidestepping the detritus of yesterday's *feria* vendors, he arrived under the leafy canopy of *El Gran Gomero*, the elephantine rubber tree beloved of porteños. Pausing to contemplate its undulating buttress roots, he noticed a small, hand-painted placard: "El gomero plantado 'en 1800' por los Hermanos Recoletos." The tree, the sign indicated, had been planted 214 years previous by members of the Order of Augustinian Recollects. Treviranus marveled at the tree that had endured for centuries. To think that it had been a sapling at around the time that Gottfried Reinhold coined the word *biology*! The Inspector cut a path toward the cemetery gates.

And then there he was: at 34° 58' S, 58° 39' W.

This was the grave of Luis Federico Leloir, an Argentine biochemist who in 1970 had received the Nobel Prize for discovering how cells metabolize lactose, milk sugar—and through his work produced an explanation of galactosemia, and lactose intolerance. A sudden wind loosed a compact leaflet up and out of the genealogy book, thwacking the Inspector in the face, as though reprimanding him for some unknown infraction. It was a 1930s pamphlet that had been authored by, of all people, Jorge Luis Borges and Adolfo Bioy Casares (who, like Borges, had been an author of fantastical tales, but who was, unlike Borges, now nearby, being, as he was, a current resident of Recoleta). Treviranus had never liked Borges; he thought the writer a troublemaker, always pressing the logical toward the illogical, in some ways like his old associate Lönnrot. Being in the labyrinth of Recoleta, it was fitting, but annoying, suddenly to be confronted with a Borges text. Leloir's mausoleum reminded the Inspector of a structure described in Borges' story, "The Circular Ruins," about a person who tries to create another person purely through dreaming, only to find that he himself is the dream of another person. More logical circularity...

But this Borges text was not so metaphysical. The pamphlet turned out, actually, to be a comically banal thing. "La leche cuajada," an essay on curdled milk, reported on the health benefits of fermented milk. "Curd cleanses the human organism; inside of the body," the two wrote, "it amplifies life."[24] Was this text another reply to "What is life?," with the answer now being… *yogurt*? The authors continued, somewhat preposterously, "El elixir de la larga vida, de los cuentos y de algunas débiles fallas de nuestra desesperanza, es por todos conocido: la leche cuajada, alimento de Matusalén." Food of Methuselah? Borges and Casares couldn't possibly have been suggesting that yogurt was the key to longevity. And yet… was it significant that Treviranus was reading this just beside the grave of Leloir? Yogurt was a form of milk that people with galactosemia could digest. It *would* amplify life, where milk could not. He thought, no coincidence, of his grandmother's undying dedication to this fermented dairy product.

This was madness. Every little fact now seemed to have magnified meaning, to close in on itself. Not everything could be connected like that. That wasn't how biology worked, was it? Were biological things entities that could attract almost any kind of phenomena into their fold, creating new unities? Or were they simply contingent collections of phenomena? Both options would bother him, though they did seem one implication of an observation offered by the great evolutionary biologist Richard Lewontin, an observation that had always stayed with him, that "there are no rigorously defined ontological 'boxes' into which biological phenomena fall, in principle."[25] That was precisely what fascinated him, but also what drove him crazy about biology—that happenstance connections were always part of the history of life, and that philosophy of biology, in its quest to be properly analytic, seemed always to be struggling to separate the contingent from the necessary, which, it was starting to appear to the Inspector, might never be foundationally possible. Life was a thing that ate its own tail, and then got distracted and started doing something else.

Now utterly perplexed, the Inspector stared at his GPS, noting that he was standing directly on the coordinates that had been so

---

24 Adolfo Bioy Casares and Jorge Luis Borges, "La leche cuajada limpia el organismo del hombre; dentro de él, ensancha su vida," in Adolfo Bioy Casares and Jorge Luis Borges, *La leche cuajada de la Martona. Estudio dietético sobre las leches* ácidas. *Folleto con recetas.* Buenos Aires: Talleres Gráficos Colón, 1935.

25 Richard Lewontin, "The Problem with Boxes," in Oren Harman and Michael R. Dietrich (eds), *Outsider Scientists: Routes to Innovation in Biology.* Chicago, IL: University of Chicago Press, 2013, pp. 349–56, here p. 349.

carefully noted in his grandmother's hand. From the corner of his eye, he saw a cat. It padded past a cluster of scarlet flowers, each one delicately arranged so that five petals radiated from a central pistil. The ornamental—a transplant from Jamaica—blossomed from a pebbled patch at the northwestern edge of Leloir's grave. Like his ancestors, the Inspector had come to know his botany. "'Treviranus appears...'" the Inspector exclaimed. "It's not Ludolph Christian Treviranus at all! And it's not Gottfried Reinhold. And it's not... me. Or *abuela*... It's this flower: *Trevirana trevirana!*"

Maybe his grandmother planted the perennial here, at Leloir's grave, a tribute to that biochemist who had studied the composition of her favorite food. Maybe she had even set to arranging this rendezvous, planting the genealogy book for him, filling it with fragments of text for him to read and puzzle over. She had counted on his curiosity, on his penchant for putting together evidence. But to what end? What was he to learn from the unlikely trail she had prepared for him to pursue? Was he meant to understand that "Treviranus appears" was not meant to designate the manifestation of a person, but rather the blossoming of a flower (named in 1809 by botanist Karl Ludwig Willdenow, it must be said, in honor of Ludolph Christian)? Was this a lesson about the arbitrary, non-identical relation between words and living things? Or was it, on the contrary, a lesson about how words (like "life," like "Treviranus") could *unify* disparate things? If the name *Treviranus* could travel from one person to another—could even leap over taxonomic boundaries to nominate a flower—well, maybe this was itself one way that living energies could travel through time, could move from animate to inanimate, from material to immaterial, and back again.

There was a more troublesome story here, too, something perhaps more world-rending than world-blending. The Inspector knew that the taxonomic name *Treviranus* had, over its history, been no small force of nomenclatural erasure. Willdenow's early nineteenth-century move to give this plant of Jamaican provenance a Latinate German name (replacing Lamarck's *Achimenes coccinea*, to which it had actually reverted in more recent years) had worked to efface the many local and Indigenous names attached to this bright red flower, samples of which, circuiting to Europe, had first been collected by botanists charged, during the height of plantation slavery in the Caribbean, with research into the economic affordances of plant life in the colonies. Some articulations of "life," it would seem, were epistemologically—and probably principally—imperialist, conceptually magnetized by the colonial search for commoditized life. What did it mean, he now reflected, that his own name, Treviranus, which followed him everywhere, pointed back to an odd Latinization of a word referring to inhabitants of Trier, Germany's oldest city, a place with which he had no special allegiance? Maybe it meant that the ghosts and lively hauntings in which his grandmother believed were—in a way even he might recognize—real.

If Treviranus remained resolutely unpersuaded of animal (or plant?) magnetism by his journey, he had become attuned to the way that the word and concept of "life" brought to itself, like a magnet, kindred and contesting stories. Looking at his compass, which now spun wildly, he thought back to the irreversible circular misfortune of Darwin Desbocatti, and mused—Life: everything points to it, and it points to everything. Death, too.

In the quickening darkness, the Inspector passed again through the gates of Recoleta. As he crossed the Plaza, he placed a hand on the rough bark of *El Gran Gomero*—this tree, this living thing, this *life*, whose majestic claws had taken root before Treviranus had even set the bearings of *biology*.

NATURE

SATURDAY, SEPTEMBER 14, 1929.

CONTENTS.

Editorial and Publishing Offices:

MACMILLAN & CO., LTD.,

ST. MARTIN'S STREET, LONDON, W.C.2.

Editorial communications should be addressed to the Editor.
Advertisements and business letters to the Publishers.

Telephone Number: GERRARD 8830.

Telegraphic Address: PHUSIS, WESTRAND, LONDON.

No. 3124, Vol. 124]

What is Life?

AT the recent South Africa meeting of the British Association there was a conference on the nature of life, at which distinguished thinkers made interesting contributions, already referred to in our columns. It may be useful to try to gather the various suggestions into a connected whole.

(1) Modern discussions of this perennial question, What is Life? have shown in varying degrees a recognition of the commonplace that an answer lies in a fuller knowledge of living creatures. No amount of verbal dexterity or even profound reflection over the concept of ' life ' floating in detachment will get us much ' forrarder ' unless we are at the same time deepening our acquaintance with organisms from microbes to men, and trying to see life whole, not as a biochemical witch-pot merely, but as the activity of individualities that develop, grow, and reproduce, that struggle, vary, and evolve. If we are to answer the question, What is Man ? or What is Personality ? we must deepen our knowledge of men and of personalities, of Shakespeare and Newton as well as of Bushmen. So to avoid false simplicity in our answer to the question, What is Life ? we must seek a comprehensive, all-round, and intimate view of organisms, taking account of intelligent apes as well as of dimly purposive amœbæ, and of psycho-biosis as well as of bio-psychosis. We cannot make sense of any kind of life without recognising the importance of fermentation, but we cannot make sense of the life of higher animals apart from feeling, intelligence, and some sort of purpose ; and the continuity of organisms makes it probable that the dim analogues of these psychical qualities are present throughout.

The extreme behaviourists or bio-mechanists, perhaps represented at the conference, to judge from the reports, by Prof. L. T. Hogben, will of course refuse to take account of any process which does not admit of physico-chemical analysis and description—a position that does not work out well in our daily life and conversation, where we have to allow at every turn for intelligent or even rational purpose—but even these extremists will agree that an understanding of life is most likely to follow a widening of our study of actual organisms.

(2) No one has as yet succeeded in re-describing in terms of anything else a fair and intact sample of that distinctive kind of activity that we call life ; and it is *possible* that the nature of life lies outside the realm of the knowable, as the non-committal Prof. Barger suggested at the conference. Such

What *Is* Life?

*Fascinating Pseudo-cells Which Display the
Non-Living Features of Protoplasm
May be Made by the Amateur
With a Few Chemicals*

By EMMA REH STEVENSON

CHOOSING for his field of research for 30 years the borderland between the inorganic and organic world of matter on the fringe of recognized science, Professor Alfonso L. Herrera, chief of the division of biology of the Mexican Department of Agriculture, has obtained curious evidence that may relate to the origin of life upon earth.

He has taken both mineral and organic substances and created from them pseudo-cells and pseudo-protoplasms that mimic life itself. His microscope has revealed imitation cells that resemble very closely those of living organisms, amœbæ, spores, streptococcus chains, bacteria, and the structure of protoplasm.

PROFESSOR HERRERA makes no extravagant claims. He merely shows that the mysterious activities of life cells and the special forms and shapes of living substance can be imitated by common mineral and organic materials that do not possess the so-called life force. He therefore believes that life is not a special phenomenon, but a property which all matter possesses under the right conditions.

Perhaps the most interesting of all of his "artificial beings," as Professor Herrera calls his imitation cells, are his "colpoids" which resemble both in appearance and in behavior the creatures called amœbæ by scientists. He treats the visitor to his laboratory

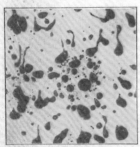

THE SECOND STAGE
One large drop breaks into rapidly moving parts which shake and tremble

to a sight of the antics of his favorite laboratory "children." He dissolves 50 parts of olive oil in 100 parts of gasoline, and 14 parts of soda lye in 100 parts of distilled water, adding a pinch of aniline black to this latter solution so that the observer can distinguish the two.

The oil-and-gasoline solution he puts into a porcelain dish with a flat bottom which he levels mechanically so that any movements in the liquid will not be due to gravity. With an

THE EXPERIMENT
The several ingredients are mixed, and a drop of the soda solution "comes to life"

eye dropper he takes a small amount of the black soda solution and inserts it under the surface of the gasoline-oil mixture. Then he hands the visitor the magnifying glass.

Almost immediately things begin to happen. The black drop becomes alive and begins to sway and tremble and shake itself. It begins to pant and breathe and divide itself into parts. These parts begin to skip around rapidly in a dissatisfied manner, pursuing, evading, and battling with other droplets for their bodies. They extend armlike appendages and fight vampire fights.

PROFESSOR A. L. HERRERA
In his laboratory at the Mexican Department of Agriculture where he experiments

They act for all the world like real single-celled living creatures going through the ordinary routine of life. They "eat" and "reproduce" like the amoeba swimming in a pond looking for its daily bread and peopling it with other amoebæ.

Professor Herrera does not claim that his oil-and-soda creatures are alive, for he can explain their strange life-like antics and amoeba-like shapes by well-known chemical and physical theories. The oil-and-soda solutions react according to the chemical process of saponification, a process the housewife used to take advantage of when she made her own soap, using rendered animal fats and leached lye from wood ashes.

WHEN a drop of the black soda solution is placed in the oil mixture, saponification immediately begins to take place around the outside of the drop, forming a thin membrane of soap around it. Then there is a black solution of one nature wrapped in a delicate bag and suspended within another solution of an entirely different disposition and character.

The soap bag which encloses the soda drop, like the membranes that envelop animal and vegetable cells in real life, is semi-permeable, and permits certain molecules to pass through. A social war of equalization takes place in an effort to make conditions on the inside of the drop more like those on the outside.

The equalization struggle is the process of saponification. Under the microscope this ordinary struggle of one solution on the outside looking in with the other one on the inside looking out, is fascinating to watch.

Tiny currents of excited material seem to be streaming through the pores of the membrane, and an active interchange of material is seen to be taking

WHAT IS LIFE?

The Greatest Puzzle of All Science Seems Today to Be Nearing a Solution . . . Yet, As it Breaks Up, its Parts in Turn Form Newer, Baffling Puzzles

By T. SWANN HARDING

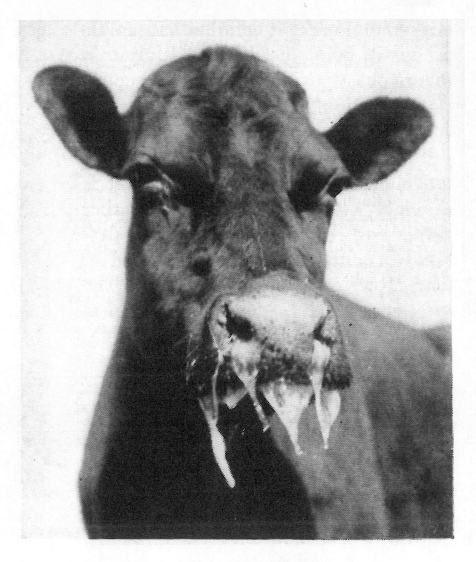

A cow, drooling at the mouth. It has hoof and mouth disease, caused by a virus. The only "cure" is to kill cattle thus infected and bury them deeply to prevent spread or a pandemic

WHAT IS LIFE?

The Physical Aspect of the Living Cell

\ BY

ERWIN SCHRÖDINGER

SENIOR PROFESSOR AT THE DUBLIN INSTITUTE FOR
ADVANCED STUDIES

WHAT IS LIFE?

The non-physicist cannot be expected even to grasp—let
alone to appreciate the relevance of—the difference in
'statistical structure' stated in terms so abstract as I have
just used. To give the statement life and colour, let me
anticipate, what will be explained in much more detail later,
namely, that the most essential part of a living cell—the
chromosome fibre—may suitably be called *an aperiodic crystal*.
In physics we have dealt hitherto only with *periodic crystals*.
To a humble physicist's mind, these are very interesting and
complicated objects; they constitute one of the most fascinating and complex material structures by which inanimate
nature puzzles his wits. Yet, compared with the aperiodic
crystal, they are rather plain and dull. The difference in
structure is of the same kind as that between an ordinary
wallpaper in which the same pattern is repeated again and
again in regular periodicity and a masterpiece of embroidery,
say a Raphael tapestry, which shows no dull repetition, but
an elaborate, coherent, meaningful design traced by the great
master.

What Is Life?

by

J. B. S. HALDANE

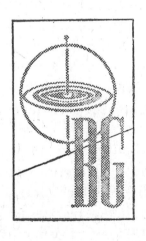

BONI AND GAER · NEW YORK

14. What Is Life?

I AM NOT GOING TO ANSWER THIS QUESTION. IN FACT, I DOUBT if it will ever be possible to give a full answer, because we know what it feels like to be alive, just as we know what redness or pain or effort are. So we cannot describe them in terms of anything else. But it is not a foolish question to ask, because we often want to know whether a man is alive or not, and when we are dealing with the microscopic agents of disease, it is clear enough that bacteria are alive, but far from clear whether viruses, such as those which cause measles and smallpox, are so.

So we have to try to describe life in terms of something else, even if the description is quite incomplete. We might try some such expression as "the influence of spirit on matter." But this would be little use for several reasons. For one thing, even if you are sure that man, and even dogs, have spirits, it needs a lot of faith to find a spirit in an oyster or a potato. For another thing, such a definition would certainly cover great works of art, or books which clearly show their author's mind, and go on influencing readers long after he is dead. Similarly it is no good trying to define life in terms of a life force. George Bernard Shaw and Professor C. E. M. Joad think there is a life force in living things. But if this has any meaning, which I doubt, you can only detect the life force in an animal or plant by its effects on matter. So we should have to define life in terms of matter. In ordinary life we recognize living things partly by their shape and texture.

BERICHTE UND MITTEILUNGEN

WAS IST LEBEN?

Der gegenwärtige Stand des Problems

von Walter Zöllner, Buenos Aires

Was ist Leben? Dies ist eine der Urfragen des menschlichen Denkens, die seit jeher Philosophen und Naturforscher gleichermaßen beschäftigt hat. Nach wie vor bleiben zwei Deutungen denkmöglich:

1. Die mechanistische Auffassung sieht im lebenden Organismus ein chemisch-physikalisches System oder — was das gleiche bedeutet — einen Mechanismus bzw. ein Zusammenspiel von Mechanismen, die sich von der unbelebten Materie prinzipiell nur durch den viel höheren Grad der Komplexheit unterscheiden. „Auch die Seele ist nur Chemie" heißt die extremste Form dieser Auffassung.

2. Die vitalistische Deutung verneint grundsätzlich, daß das Phänomen des Lebens mit einer mechanistischen Betrachtungsweise erschöpfend beschrieben werden kann, da die Zielstrebigkeit, das Selbstschaffen, die schöpferische Potenz des Organismus in seiner Ganzheit auf diesem Wege nicht erfaßt wird. Der Vitalismus führt deshalb einen „Vitalfaktor" (Driesch) ein, welcher als wesentliche Kraft das ganze System des Organismus überhaupt erst zum Funktionieren bringt.

Wie Meyer-Abich in seinem Aufsatz über Driesch (Band I, S. 356 dieser Ztschr.) ganz klar feststellte, ist diese vitalistische Auffassung erstmals bei Aristoteles in der Idee der Entelechie klar und prägnant ausgesprochen worden, und jeder Vitalismus wird daher stets „eine Renaissance der Biologie und organischen Philosophie des Aristoteles" sein. Ferner handelt es sich bei dem modernen, von Driesch gegründeten Vitalismus um eine wirkliche schöpferische Renaissance und nicht um eine bloße Aufwärmung von Gedankengängen aus der griechischen Philosophie.

Hier muß eine grundsätzliche Einschaltung über die Wiederaufnahme sogenannter Urprobleme oder Letztfragen des menschlichen Denkens gemacht werden: Man trifft heute immer wieder auf die Behauptung, daß all unser modernes Forschen doch nur wieder auf die uralten Weisheiten der griechischen Philosophen zurückführe, daß von ihnen alle Ergebnisse schon vorweggenommen seien, nichts grundsätzlich Neues mehr gedacht werden könne. Vielfach schwingt bei solchen Feststellungen noch das stolze Gefühl der eigenen umfassenden Kenntnisse mit, wobei man den alten Philosophen gewissermaßen wohlwollend auf die Schultern klopft, daß es doch erstaunlich sei, wie gut die klassischen Herren mit ihren primitiven Forschungsmitteln die modernen Auffassungen vorausahnen konnten (im ähnlichen Sinne, wie man dies heute mit Jules Verne und seinen technischen Zukunftsromanen zu tun pflegt).

Tatsächlich bestand die ungeheure Leistung der griechischen Philosophie unter anderem auch in dem Auffinden und Durchdenken fast aller Denkmöglichkeiten, welche in den einzelnen, oft konträren Systemen und Schulen gleichwertig nebeneinander bestanden. Tatsächlich scheint es auch so, als ob die Urproblemstellungen von der griechischen Philosophie erschöpfend erfaßt worden seien.

生命とは何か

田宮　博・川喜田愛郎
岡　小天・務臺理作

アテネ文庫
— 70 —

弘文堂

SECCION PARAMEDICA
MECANICA CLASICA Y MECANICA BIOLOGICA
¿QUE ES LA VIDA?

por

ANTONIO GARCIA VALCARCEL

Tras no pequeños esfuerzos y después de múltiples y, según mi propio juicio, vanos intentos, he ido situándome, a lo largo de mi vida, como a caballo sobre esa real o aparente barrera que separa el mundo físico-químico, inorgánico o inanimado, de nuestro mundo biológico, objeto preferente de nuestros afanes como médicos. Y en esta posición —con sus posibles ventajas subjetivas, por parecerme que desde ella se divisan más amplios horizontes y reales y amplias comunicaciones entre ambos campos, y con sus seguros inconvenientes y peligros, puesto que a medida que se agrande nuestro campo de observación, es más difícil percibir con detalle y acierto la realidad— me siento verdaderamente incómodo, aunque, sin duda, merecidamente. Porque si pretendo comunicar mis impresiones a los físicos, aún cuando hallen razonable mi exposición, encuentran que empleo un lenguaje «semibárbaro». Un ilustre profesor de Físico-Química, me decía —creo que todo sinceridad—, a la vez que me recomendaba la exposición de mis ideas en un centro superior: «Dice usted cosas que pueden ser interesantes, pero emplea un lenguaje tan poco técnico que resulta verdaderamente chocante». Otros físicos me indicaron la conveniencia o necesidad de que concretara mis ideas en expresiones matemáticas, único idioma que —no sin graves motivos— aceptan como oficial en esta ciencia. ¡Pobre de mí! Es casi como si me pidieran que —¡yo, que apenas si distingo las siete notas de la escala!— trasladara al pentagrama el «Septimino» que, sin conocer Música, soy capaz de entonar con bastante aproximación. Si después de escuchar las opiniones de los físicos, no adversas, aún cuando reservadas, pretendo dirigirme a los biólogos, pronto siento sobre mí, explícita o implícitamente, la pregunta inevitable: ¿Qué tiene que ver todo esto con la Biología? Este recelo me parece perfectamente justificado; porque, ciertamente, para pedir a mis interlocutores o lectores el esfuerzo que ha de representarles el seguir mis razonamientos, supone el concederme un margen de confianza que, con toda lógica, no es fácil otorgarme, aun cuando la benevolencia y la amplitud de criterio de MEDICINA ESPAÑOLA, me lo haya concedido hasta aquí. Mas como todos los anteriores artículos sólo viene a cons-

SCIENCE IN REVIEW

Reconstruction of Virus in Laboratory Reopens the Question: What Is Life?

By WALDEMAR KAEMPFFERT

Last September Dr. Harry Commoner of Washington University, St. Louis, Mo., rose at the Minneapolis meeting of the American Chemical Society to relate how he and his colleagues, Eddie Basler Jr., Tung-Yue Wang and James A. Lippincott, had torn a virus apart, put the dead parts together again and restored infective activity. This was reported in this department on Sept. 18. The work had been done only a month previously so that the investigators had no time to deal with the subject thoroughly. In his paper Dr. Commoner referred to similar work done by Drs. Heinz I. Fraenkel-Conrat and Dr. Robley Williams of the University of California's Virus Laboratory, of which Dr. Wendell M. Stanley, Nobel Laureate, is the head.

Now come the Californians with a complete paper which appears in the current Proceedings of the National Academy of Sciences and which was submitted in June, two months before Dr. Commoner and his colleagues obtained their preliminary results. Moreover, the work done in the University of California in March was thorough. Every chemical phase was explored.

Any scientist who claims that he has torn a virus apart, killed it and then put it together again with complete reactivity must expect a raising of skeptical eyebrows. Drs. Fraenkel-Conrat and Williams knew it, for which reason they repeated their experiments over and over again and discussed them with small groups of virologists.

Basis of Life

In appraising this achievement it must be borne in mind that nucleic acids and proteins constitute the basis of life. The two are chemically united in bacteria and in viruses. Years ago Dr. Stanley split the nucleic acids from the proteins. But what is the relationship of the two? This question has been answered by Drs. Fraenkel-Conrat and Williams.

Nucleic acids come in the form of strands which run through rods of protein, like lead through a pencil. But the rod is coiled, not straight. The coil can be broken down and recombined into long rods of proteins alone. These look like viruses but are not infectious because they contain no nucleic acid. At this point Drs. Fraenkel-Conrat and Williams enter. They succeeded in combining the fragments of protein with what is called "native" nucleic acid—so-called because it is found in the nuclei of cells. But was the recombination an active virus? There was one critical test, and that was to rub the recombination on leaves of the tobacco plant. (It was the virus of the tobacco virus disease with which the experiments were made.) Separated, the proteins and the nucleic acid had no effect; combined they produced the blight known as tobacco virus disease.

LA SPIRALE: DIRETTIVA BIOLOGICA DELLA VITA

CHE COSA È LA VITA?

(Saggio di filosofia biologica)

Dott. LAMBERTO VITALE

> *La mia dottrina può non essere vera,*
> *ma sembra però verosimile.*
>
> SENOFANE

Quando muore un nostro parente, oppure una persona con la quale siamo legati da vincoli di affetto, spesso ci chiediamo: che cosa è mai la vita? L'avvenimento irreparabile della morte, per la sua stessa natura e per un curioso contrasto ci richiama alla nostra mente ed alla nostra considerazione l'essenza della vita.

Il veloce turbinio della vita vissuta in quest'epoca di civiltà meccanicizzata non consente alla nostra coscienza che delle rare pause per concentrare il pensiero su ploblemi metafisici e che non siano di immediato interesse pratico come è, appunto, il tema che sto trattando. Si pensa, perciò, alla vita quando il suo opposto, la morte, è là a testimoniare la sua inesorabile presenza.

Non sarà inutile, spero, affrontare questo problema ora che nè io e nè, mi auguro, i lettori siamo sotto il deprimente influsso di un evento luttuoso. Dovremmo avere, anzi, appunto per ciò, la mente più serena: io ad esporre e voi che leggete a seguire la mia teoria.

L'argomento è senza alcun dubbio molto interessante e già Aristotele suppose che la vita fosse insita nel *principio perfettibile*, mentre Platone credette vederla nell'*anima teologica attiva* ed i teologi pensarono facesse parte dei *disegni imperscrutabili* dell'Ente divino.

A cominciare dagli antichi filosofi della Scuola ionica fino ai tempi moderni si è tentato di spiegare il fenomeno della vita ora con una concezione *meccanicista* ora con una concezione *vitalista*. Meccanicismo e vitalismo, pertanto, costituiscono due termini antitetici che designano due concezioni biologiche diametralmente opposte.

In breve: il *meccanicismo* nell'interpretazione dei fenomeni della vita esclude ogni elemento psichico e li riduce a processi fisici, chimici, meccanici, regolati unicamente da leggi che vengono studiate dalle scienze fisico-chimiche. Il *vitalismo*, al contrario, fonda la sua interpretazione della vita sull'elemento teleologico, vale a dire su di una finalità (insita in ogni atto fenomenico) che viene guidata da una entità immateriale (che può essere l'anima o lo spirito vitale), sia immanente che trascendente, comunque indipendente da fenomeni chimico-fisici.

Sarebbe una faccenda lunga e noiosa tracciare qui la storia di queste concezioni biologiche. Basti ricordare le principali teorie: tra quelle *statiche* (che cioè considerano la materia dal solo punto di vista morfologico) la teoria di

karel honzík
co je životní sloh

svazek

5   československý spisovatel

And Say the Fossil Responded?

I was, for a time, lucky enough to greet an ancient metaorganism every morning on my way to work. Sunning itself in the corner of a long, glassed-in hallway beside a stump of petrified wood, the unassuming stone was roughly the color, silhouette, and size of an elderly tortoise, domed and saddle-backed, though it moved even more slowly. Oftentimes, I would pass it (my impulse is to call it "them") in the early morning to discover that it had been sullied in the night, as cleaning staff would balance a blue plastic recycling bin on its uppermost cuticle after emptying the day's paper waste. For the better half of a semester, an abandoned coffee thermos perched on the stone; late in the year, it would be obscured beneath a shoal of discarded exam booklets.

I felt as if the stone and I shared an understanding, because in 2014 I had begun to immerse myself as an anthropologist in the work and worlds of geobiologists, scientists who study the coevolution of biological life and planetary history across spans of deep time. Having learned from geobiologists how to look for and think about fossils that predate the Cambrian explosion 542 million years ago, I could readily identify this particular stone as a stromatolite, the fossilized body of a once-living bacterial mat that had lived and flourished, breathed and metabolized and, eventually, congealed into a concrete bulwark against the wave action of an alkaline sea billions of years before anything like plant or animal life first arose. Stromatolites are the only ancient fossils visible to the naked eye; they are in some respects similar to contemporary coral reefs, if those reefs had been built eons ago, by microbes instead of animals, and on a pale young planet entirely alien to our contemporary world. If you were to cut the entire history of Earth in half, the stromatolite lived and died closer in time to the formation of the solar system than to me.

What I'm saying is that the stone gave me perspective. So much so that after a few years it began to occupy an outsize role in my psychic landscape and, as can happen in such cases, appeared to me in dreams. These dreams would begin more or less the same as my waking mornings, sun slanting into the hallway, stromatolite degraded by the detritus of higher education. The dream would only reveal itself as such when I spoke to the stromatolite, and it duly responded. The conversation, by my lights, rarely varied, and ran roughly as follows:

Me: "Stromatolite! Why do you allow yourself to be treated
this way! You don't deserve this. Why don't you tell anyone that
you're a magnificent ancient being?"
Stromatolite: "Maybe the reason I've endured this long is because no one recognizes that I'm remarkable."

If I had had the lucidity to do so, I might have asked the stromatolite
other sorts of questions, given how intimately its history is imbricated
in the search for both the origins of life on Earth and evidence that life
has flourished elsewhere. And what if I had asked the stromatolite,
"What is life?." And say the fossil responded?[1]
    I'm not the first person to whom a stromatolite has spoken, but
to the best of my knowledge it's been a while. In 1859, the rock beneath
the Cambrian stratum was not called pre-Cambrian, it was simply
known as "Azoic" rock because it was universally believed that no life
could possibly be found there. As a deep past for both the planet and
all life on it began to shade in scientific circles from possibility into
probability, the Azoic of course posed a problem. Darwin acknowl-
edged that the absence of fossils in this stratum was among the central
weaknesses of his thesis in *On the Origin of Species*:

> [I]f my theory be true, it is indisputable that before the lowest
> Silurian stratum was deposited, long periods elapsed [...]
> and that during these vast, yet quite unknown, periods of time,
> the world swarmed with living creatures. To the question
> why we do not find records of these vast primordial periods,
> I can give no satisfactory answer.[2]

Serendipitously, the same year Darwin was ruminating on the gap in
the fossil record, a solution presented itself to geologist William
Dawson of McGill University while he was examining Azoic rocks that
had been mailed to him by a collector for the Geological Survey of
Canada. He discerned in the putatively lifeless limestone something

---

1   Jacques Derrida, *The Animal That Therefore I Am*, ed. Marie-Louise Mallet,
    trans. David Wills. New York: Fordham University Press, 2008,
    pp. 199-240.
2   Charles Darwin, *On the Origin of Species by Means of Natural Selection,
    or the Preservation of Favoured Races in the Struggle for Life*. London: John
    Murray, 1859, pp. 306-07.

curiously lifelike, and so named the newly discovered fossil, which he believed to be the progenitor of all life on Earth, Eozoön canadense (the "Dawn Animal of Canada"). While it would be more than a century before some specimens of Eozoön would be identified as stromatolites,[3] Dawson was certain that he had found the most primitive life-form on Earth, a massive foraminifer that had thickly coated the seafloor. Eozoön homodiegetically narrates Dawson's 1875 report:

> I, Eozoon Canadense [sic], being a creature of low organization and intelligence, and of practical turn, am no theorist, but have a lively appreciation of such facts as I am able to perceive. I found myself growing upon the sea-bottom, and know not when I came. I grew and flourished for ages, and found no let or hindrance to my expansion, and abundance of food was always floated to me without my having to go in search of it. [...] I have done my best to avoid extinction; but it is clear that I must at length be overcome, and must either disappear or subside into a humbler condition, and that other creatures better provided for the new conditions of the world must take my place.[4]

Darwin was among those thrilled by the news of life's newfound antiquity, devoting a passage of a later edition of *Origin* to Eozoön: "within the last year the great discovery of the Eozoon in the Laurentian formation of Canada has been made; and after reading Dr. Carpenter's description of this remarkable fossil, it is impossible to feel any doubt regarding its organic nature."[5] Perhaps William Thomson (1st Baron, Lord Kelvin) had Eozoön in mind when, in his 1871 Presidential Address to the British Association for the Advancement of Science, he mused about life's extraterrestrial origin, "we must regard it as probable in the highest degree that there are countless seed-bearing

---

3   Many of Dawson's samples were later recognized to be abiotic. See Charles F. O'Brien, *"Eozoön Canadense* 'The Dawn Animal of Canada,'" *Isis*, vol. 61, no. 2 (1970), pp. 206–23.

4   John W. Dawson, *The Dawn of Life: Being the History of the Oldest Known Fossil Remains, and Their Relations to Geological Time and to the Development of the Animal Kingdom*. Montreal: Dawson Brothers, 1875, pp. 229–30.

5   Charles Darwin, *On the Origin of Species by Means of Natural Selection, or the Preservation of Favoured Races in the Struggle for Life*, 4th ed. London: John Murray, 1866, p. 371.

meteoric stones moving about through space. If at the present instant no life existed upon this Earth, one such stone falling upon it might, by what we blindly call natural causes, lead to its becoming covered with vegetation."[6] Perhaps, then, "life [has actually] originated on this Earth through moss-grown fragments from the ruins of another world."[7] Might these extraterrestrial "moss-grown fragments" be akin to stromatolitic Eozoön?

That possibility certainly was not lost on Otto Hahn, a German petrologist and ardent advocate of Emanuel Swedenborg's astrotheology, who travelled to Canada to sample limestone outcrops alongside Dawson. At first a hard-boiled skeptic, Hahn over time grew increasingly convinced that Dawson's Eozoön samples were in fact the petrified remains of an originary form of life, though Hahn believed this Ur-creature to have been floral (and hence renamed it "Eophylum"). Upon returning to Germany, Hahn devoted himself to studying chondrite (that is, non-metallic) meteorites, using the new technique of photomicrography to capture the fossilized extraterrestrial life-forms he viewed in thin-section, which he believed to be akin to Eophylum and the likely origin of all life on Earth:

> However, in my study of twenty chondrites (and 360 thin sections of them) the assertion made in my Urzelle was confirmed—that the rock of the chondrites is not a type of sedimentary rock as on Earth, in which fossils are embedded, that it is not a conglomerate formation; but rather, its whole mass is entirely formed of organic beings, like our coral rocks. So not a plant, as I had assumed earlier, but plant-animals! *The whole stone is life.*[8]

6   William Thomson, "Inaugural Address to the British Association at Edinburgh," *Nature*, vol. 4, no. 92 (1871), pp. 261–78, here p. 270.
7   Anonymous, "What is Life?," *The Lawrence Daily Journal*, March 1, 1898, p. 16.
8   "Nun bestätigte sich aber auch bei meiner Untersuchung von 20 Chondriten (und 360 Dünnschliffen davon) die in meiner *Urzelle* aufgestellte Behauptung, dass das Gestein der Chondrite nicht etwa nach Art der Sedimentgesteine unserer Erde nur ein Schlamm sei, in welchen die Versteinerungen eingelagert sind, dass es nicht eine Konglomeratbildung sei; ihre ganze Masse ist vielmehr völlig aus organischen Wesen gebildet, wie unsere Korallenfelsen. Also keine Pflanze, wie ich früher annahm, aber Pflanzentiere! Und der ganze Stein ein Leben."
     See Otto Hahn, *Die Meteorite (Chondrite) und ihre Organismen*. Tübingen: Verlag der H. Laupp'schen Buchhandlung, 1880 (emphasis added).

Micrographic-thin sections of meteorite fragments,
from Otto Hahn

As I delved deeper into Dawson and Hahn's papers on Eozoön, seeking
to chart the history of the search for the origin of life in the geological
record, my encounters with stromatolites grew increasingly frequent.
On holiday in Vienna, I detoured to the bathroom on my way out of
the Naturhistorisches Museum, having spent the afternoon wandering in Maria Theresa's Enlightenment collections.[9] Skirting an empty
hall, I stopped short before a stromatolite, its laminae meandering
across its lustrous surface. Beside it, a collection cabinet was labeled
with a surprising question—not "What is life?" but "Why is life?"
("Warum Leben?"). Who, I wondered, was asking?

      That fall, after I had interviewed a geobiology professor, he
offered me unlimited access to his rock archive. On odd mornings, I
would make a pilgrimage across the street to poke around, finding

9   See Naturhistorisches Museum Wien, "Museum of Enlightenment,"
    https://www.nhm-wien.ac.at/en/museum/history_architecture
    /museum_of_enlightenment, last accessed May 3, 2021.

one day a vial of lunar dust from Apollo 11, on another a hunk of the Gunflint chert, a banded ironstone shot through with jasper, delicately wrapped in tissue paper. This stromatolite, then known as Cryptozoon, was first hammered from its outcrop in the summer of 1952. While on a trip prospecting for iron ore in Lake Ontario, mineralogist Stanley Tyler had taken a day off to go trout fishing. From the bow of his canoe he noticed Cryptozoon interbedded with jet-black cherts. Upon returning to his laboratory in Madison, Wisconsin, Tyler found that under the microscope the samples he'd hammered off the outcrop abounded with microscopic life-forms that had flash-frozen in silica two billion years prior. This was the first modern compelling physical evidence of Precambrian cellular life. Tyler had, in his words, "glimpse[d] through the Precambrian metamorphic veil."[10] The ancient planet had, as Darwin once surmised, "swarmed with living creatures," and stromatolites had now disclosed an abundant archive of life, long preceding the Cambrian: single-celled ancestors invisible without the aid of a diamond knife and a light microscope. Within a decade, Tyler's breathtaking discovery, which would be co-published and further researched posthumously with the help of his collaborator Elso Barghoorn, would ground the new subdiscipline of geobiology.[11]

In the 1960s, geobiologists, a cadre of field scientists working at the intersection of the earth and life sciences, began to seek out further ancient fossils in hopes of better understanding how life originated on Earth and evolved in the context of changing planetary atmospheres. Suddenly, stromatolites seemed to stud every Precambrian sedimentary rock, and geobiologists sought them in the world's most ancient unmetamorphosed formations—the Warrawoona and Strelley Pool Groups in Western Australia, the Onverwacht Group in Swaziland, in Southern Africa, at Woman Lake in Northwestern

10 J. William Schopf, *Cradle of Life: The Discovery of Earth's Earliest Fossils.* Princeton, NJ: Princeton University Press, 2001, p. 38.

11 See Stanley A. Tyler and Elso S. Barghoorn, "Occurrence of Structurally Preserved Plants in Pre-Cambrian Rocks of the Canadian Shield," *Science*, vol. 119, no. 3096 (1954), pp. 606-08; Elso S. Barghoorn and Stanley A. Tyler, "Microorganisms from the Gunflint Chert," *Science*, vol. 147, no. 3658 (1965), pp. 563-77; and Preston E. Cloud, "Significance of the Gunflint (Precambrian) Microflora," *Science*, vol. 148, no. 3666 (1965), pp. 27-28.

Canada; they compared these primordial microbial mounds to extant mats brooding in the Bahamas, Mexico, and Australia.[12]

When NASA launched its inquiry into the possibility of life beyond Earth in 1964, geobiologists were among those scientists first tasked with determining the scientific value of looking for life on Mars. Is it, they inquired, worthwhile to "approach the prospect of Martian exploration as evolutionary biologists" in order to test the hypothesis that "the origin of living organization is a probable event in the evolution of all planetary crusts that resemble ours"?[13] In the first chapter of the resulting report, entitled "What is Life?," Daniel Mazia, a Berkeley cell biologist who had first identified the mitotic spindle, fixed on traces of biotic form to answer his title question. Scientists may be able, he argued, to "deduce from fossil shadows the forms and ways of life of organisms that have long ago surrendered survival to durability. [...] Complex forms are always taken seriously as signs of living things. We can be moved by fossil forms and find a singular beauty in form that is congealed in time."[14]

While it may at first seem that the search for life on other planets might demand a universalizing, decontextualized, or formal definition of life, these inquiries into extraterrestrial life were not context-independent. Rather, informed by geobiological thinking that life is a phenomenon inextricable from and mutually constitutive of planetary history, they began with more modest questions about geological and climatological contexts—less what, and more where and when is life? Working within the premise that the organic and

12 See J. William Schopf, "Microflora of the Bitter Springs Formation, Late Precambrian, Central Australia," *Journal of Paleontology*, vol. 42, no. 3 (1968), pp. 651-88; Andrew H. Knoll, Elso S. Barghoorn, and Stjepko Golubić, "Paleopleurocapsa Wopfnerii Gen. et sp. nov.: A Late Precambrian Alga and Its Modern Counterpart," *Proceedings of the National Academy of Sciences*, vol. 72, no. 7 (1975), pp. 2488-92; Andrew H. Knoll and Elso S. Barghoorn, "A Gunflint-Type Microbiota from the Duck Creek Dolomite, Western Australia," *Origins of Life*, vol. 7, no. 4 (1976), pp. 417-23; and Hans J. Hofmann, "Precambrian Remains in Canada: Fossils, Dubiofossils, and Pseudofossils," *International Geological Congress 24th Session*, nos 20-30 (1972), p. 27.

13 National Research Council, *Biology and the Exploration of Mars*. Washington, DC: National Academies Press, 1966, p. 8.

14 Daniel Mazia, "What is Life?," in National Research Council, *Biology and the Exploration of Mars*, pp. 23-40, here p. 30.

inorganic form one another in a manner that renders the two at times indistinct across geological epochs, scientists seeking to develop a theory of life on other Earth-like planets did not fully abstract definitions of life. Instead, they conceptualized life as symptomatic of certain kinds of planetary histories. Life was a phenomenon involved, convolved in its very planetary contexts.

It was at this same NASA meeting that chemist James Lovelock began formulating the Gaia hypothesis, for which he joined forces with evolutionary biologist Lynn Margulis. In its earliest iteration, Lovelock posited that if life had ever existed on Mars, then one sign of life would be modifications in the gas composition of that planet's atmosphere. Because no such signal was detectable, he thought he could save the American taxpayer a good deal of money. More provocatively, he and Margulis together posited that life was a planetary event, that "Earth's atmosphere is [...] produced by the biosphere for the biosphere."[15] Earth's biosphere, notably, first radically deviated from its steady-state condition, shifting from a reducing to an oxidizing environment, most likely because of the collective action and abundance of stromatolites, which would star in Margulis and Lovelock's first paper outlining their Gaia hypothesis.[16]

Margulis was captivated by stromatolites and their descendants, living microbial mats.[17] With paleontologist Stanley Awramik, she would draft the modern biogenic definition of a stromatolite in 1974: "Stromatolites are megascopic organosedimentary structures produced by sediment trapping, binding, and/or precipitation as a result of growth and metabolic activity of organisms, primarily blue-green algae."[18] She likened them to "magic carpets" because they

15 Lynn Margulis and James E. Lovelock, "Atmospheres and Evolution," in
    John Billingham (ed.), *Life in the Universe*. Cambridge, MA: MIT Press,
    1981, pp. 79–100, here p. 96.
16 Lynn Margulis and James E. Lovelock. "Biological Modulation of the Earth's
    Atmosphere," *Icarus*, vol. 21, no. 4 (1974), pp. 471–89.
17 Stefan Helmreich, "Sippewissett Time-Slip," in Dorion Sagan (ed.), *Lynn
    Margulis: The Life and Legacy of a Scientific Rebel*. White River Junction,
    VT: Chelsea Green, 2012, pp. 97–102.
18 Stanley Awramik and Lynn Margulis, *Stromatolite Newsletter* (unpublished),
    February 1974, p. 5, quoted from M. R. Walter (ed.), *Stromatolites:
    Developments in Sedimentology* 20. New York: Elsevier, 1976, p. 1.

"have the power to take scientists back in time," more than three billion years deep into the Archean.[19] Over the course of more than forty years studying microbial mats, she understood them to be bacterial fabrics of densely intertwined microbial filaments "merging metabolic talents" such that cyanobacteria thrive on their sticky surfaces while odder guilds of fermenters and reducers bed down in the interior.[20] She viewed in these companionate mergers early evidence for both the Gaia hypothesis and for endosymbiosis, the concept that complex life is an artifact of ongoing intimate biological partnerships and mergers rather than "nature, red in tooth and claw." As cyanobacteria slip sunward, trapped sediment and sand clot the mats such that, in the fullness of time, architectonic domes spindrift, spume into stone. When Margulis and her son Dorion Sagan later asked, "So, what is life?" one answer was stromatolites: "Undercover and unwitnessed, life back then was the prodigious progeny of bacteria. It still is."[21]

Fossilized microbial mats seam inquiries into the origins of life on Earth to related questions about whether it is likely that life emerged elsewhere. Attending an astrobiology conference in Washington, DC, I palmed an Archean sandstone from the Strelley Pool Formation in Western Australia while listening to an astrobiologist talk about "exotic biochemistries." Strelley Pool, whose stromatolites are the oldest known fossils on Earth, is now studied as a proxy for Martian lithology, as its stromatolites are of the same age as the Noachian outcrops explored first by the Curiosity rover and more lately by the Perseverance rover. Indeed, several key scientists on the NASA Mars 2020 rover mission, chartered to seek ancient fossilized or biochemical evidence of extraterrestrial life, first trained at Strelley Pool. In anticipation of the 2020 mission, planetary scientists, geobiologists, and astrobiologists published papers hypothesizing the likelihood of Jezero Crater harboring stromatolitic rocks and asked, if such fossils are extant, how they might best be detected.

19 Lynn Margulis and Dorion Sagan, *What is Life?* New York: Simon and Schuster, 1995, p. 86.
20 Ibid.
21 Ibid., p. 89.

In a NASA site selection workshop in 2017, Ken Williford, Deputy Scientist for the mission, summarized how NASA and Jet Propulsion Laboratory (JPL) scientists narrowed down more than 130 potential Martian landing sites, explaining that the best chances of finding signs of past life on Mars is by studying Martian regions that are analogous to earthly geobiological field sites: "Where do stromatolites form?" he asked his colleagues, and recommended that they seek out "astrobiologically-relevant Martian analog environments," such as the 3.49 billion-year-old Dresser Formation and the 3.42 billion-year-old Strelley Pool Formation, both part of the Pilbara Supergroup in Western Australia whose stromatolites had first lured geobiologists in the 1960s and 1970s. Two other planetary scientists summarized their exploration strategy simply as "look for the microbial mats." Indeed, 3.5 billion years ago, Jezero Crater, the locality ultimately selected for the sampling mission, was flooded by river channels inundating a massive caldera to form a deep lake. NASA scientists explicitly selected Jezero because it is a proxy, not for extant Earth ecosystems, but for ancient environments whose lithified organic remains are now sampled by geobiologists.[22]

One hundred and fifty years after William Thomson, Lord Kelvin's inaugural address, Perseverance tooled around an ancient Martian lake bed scouting for "moss-grown fragments from the ruins of another world."[23] In their published report, Mars 2020-participating earth and life scientists asked, "What is a martian [sic] biosignature? Will we know it when we see it? [...] we may consider the astrobiological 'holy grail' of a Mars rover mission to be something like a stromatolite—a finely layered sedimentary rock that may represent a fossil microbial mat."[24]

22 For an analysis of the practices by which NASA scientists come to see earthly places as proxies for extraterrestrial topographies, see Lisa Messeri, *Placing Outer Space: An Earthly Ethnography of Other Worlds*. Durham, NC: Duke University Press, 2016.
23 Thomson, "Inaugural Address to the British Association at Edinburgh."
24 Kenneth H. Williford et al., "The NASA Mars 2020 Rover Mission and the Search for Extraterrestrial Life," in Nathalie Cabrol and Edmond Grin (eds), *From Habitability to Life on Mars*. Cambridge, MA: Elsevier, 2018, pp. 275–308, here p. 296.

trapping

What might explain the endurance of such a self-admittedly "unremarkable" rock in inquiries into life's origin, uniqueness, and ubiquity? Recall Margulis likening a stromatolite to a "magic carpet," a kind of time-travelling machine or wormhole that can launch earth and life scientists into the deep past of life on Earth. In this sense, stromatolites are vehicles that gather together two things that are otherwise distant—whether in space, time, or discourse. Borrowing Paul Ricoeur's description of the living or live metaphor (la métaphore vive), they draw difference into propinquity by recognizing and making manifest a kinship that is otherwise obscured. Good metaphors take you somewhere (or somewhen) else, like the Greek buses Michel de Certeau mentions in *The Practice of Everyday Life*: "To go to work or come home, one takes a 'metaphor'—a bus or a train."[25] With tropic force, stromatolites pitch geologists from present-day Quintana Roo to the Pilbara Craton during the Paleoarchaean Eon 3.4 billion years ago, from the Pilbara to the Perseverance rover, and from the Perseverance rover to the Noachian Period on a young Mars.[26]

When listening to the question "What is life?" as a leitmotif in the life sciences, sometimes it is profitable to worry less about the predicate and more about the verb. Implicit in every metaphor is deliberate comparison, and "the 'place' of metaphor, its most intimate and ultimate abode, is [...] the copula of the verb to be."[27] And so, if the stromatolite had responded, perhaps it would have reminded me that asking "What is life?" necessarily poses other, unspoken but inferred questions: "What is not life?" and "What is life like?" Perhaps we may think of stromatolites, then, as living metaphors of life, innovating new meanings of what life might be by making proximate entities that are otherwise remote. The latent metaphoricity of "is" is also a reminder that such questions, more than being idle, make

25 Michel de Certeau, *The Practice of Everyday Life*. Berkeley, CA: University of California Press, 1984, p. 115. On the tropological and topological effects of metaphor, see also Melody Jue, *Wild Blue Media: Thinking Through Seawater*. Durham, NC: Duke University Press, 2020.

26 Here I mean "tropic" both in the sense of something that is rhetorical or figurative and in the sense of directed movement, as when photosynthetic organisms are "heliotropic," growing sunward.

27 Paul Ricoeur, *The Rule of Metaphor*. New York: Routledge, 2003, p. 6.

manifest new meanings and forms of life, new ways in which certain kinds of life and lives come to matter. On this reading, the question "What is life?" engenders not only a biopoetics, or discourse about life, but also a biopoiesis—the sort of complex and relational ecologies in which things like microbial mats thrive and, in so doing, further reinvigorate the ecological conditions that made them possible. In all life, as in discourse, meaning manifests not in texts, but in contexts.[28]

28 "Sympoiesis is a word proper to complex, dynamic, responsive, situated, historical systems. It is a word for worlding-with, in company. Sympoiesis enfolds autopoiesis and generatively unfurls and extends it." See Donna Haraway, *Staying with the Trouble: Making Kin in the Chthulucene*. Durham, NC: Duke University Press, 2016, p.58.

WHAT IS LIFE?

By RENÉ BIOT, M.D.

Translated from the French by ERIC EARNSHAW SMITH

HAWTHORN BOOKS · PUBLISHERS · *New York*

CHAPTER II

)

LIVING DUST

"Life is but a word meaning ignorance. When we apply the adjective 'living' to anything, we mean merely that we are dealing with a phenomenon of whose immediate cause and conditions we are ignorant."

This is the language of scepticism, the words of a disillusioned man looking back over a lifetime wasted in biological research. Yet they were written by Claude Bernard himself, the father of modern physiology, in his *Introduction à l'étude de la médecine expérimentale,* and in a paragraph pungently sub-titled: "Scientific ignorance combined with certain illusions of the medical outlook are an obstacle to the progress of experimental medicine."

Bernard was obviously preoccupied with this problem, to which he frequently returned; no doubt because it seemed to him even more important than all those more tangible problems which his experimental genius had succeeded in solving. His naturally speculative turn of mind—well illustrated in his photograph by Trinquart—was constantly reverting to the ultimate question: what is life?

COUNTERACTING THE DECOMPOSITION OF MATTER

The formula which we quoted above—"life is death"—is contradicted by another, equally well known and infinitely suggestive. It was employed by Bichat, whose short life (he

CHAPTER 1

WHAT IS LIFE?

DANIEL MAZIA

We do not seek to evade the question of the nature of life, but perhaps we should, with stricter discipline, speak rather of living things, organisms, biological objects or the like. For these things exist and they are distinctive among things in general. Biology, in common sense and in formal science, may be unrigorous but it is not imbecilic. It is not trivial that we distinguish corals from rocks, babies from dolls, know when to call the doctor and when to call the undertaker. To say that we cannot answer the question "What is Life?" may imply only that we have no simple predicate for the sentence beginning "Life is . . .". That may be a statement of fact, namely that we now believe that the intuitive hypotheses that life is a special "something," a special force or a magic substance, are scientifically incorrect. This experience is not unique in science; the discrediting of the phlogiston theory wiped out the pat definitions of fire and heat, but we did not for that reason deny fire and heat. Perhaps we should not speak of a definition at all. Our task is rather to identify those properties—forms, substances, processes—that are comprehended in the idea of life. The longer the statement, the better, if length is a measure not of prolixity but of the number of features common to living things and distinguishing them from other kinds of things. Such an experimental approach—it is an experiment to see whether the facts of life define life—cannot pretend to satisfy the desire for a more analytical and purely logical approach, but at

25

▮ QU'EST-CE QUE LA VIE

par le Pr DELAUNAY,
Chef du Service de pathologie expérimentale
de l'Institut de Garches

Mesdames, Messieurs,

Rien n'est plus simple que de distinguer un être vivant, par exemple une bactérie, un de ces animaux dont nous parlait Monsieur Bressou, et même l'homme, d'un objet inanimé. D'un autre côté les biologistes n'ont eu aucun mal à déterminer les caractères qui signent l'être vivant. Il s'agit, vous le savez, de la sensibilité, de la motilité, du pouvoir d'assimilation, du pouvoir de reproduction, ou de cette évolution qui fait que nous naissons, et que nous grandissons, et enfin que nous mourons. Mais quand il s'agit de définir non pas ce qu'est un être vivant mais ce qu'est la vie elle-même, c'est une toute autre histoire.

Bien sûr il existe dans la littérature d'innombrables définitions de la vie, certaines même sont très simples. Tolstoï à qui on demandait : Qu'est-ce que la vie ? se contentait de répondre : La vie ... c'est la vie.

A Definition Is Debated: Exactly What Is 'Life'?

...It's the most interesting form of organization of matter on Earth —'the activity of a biosphere'

by Gerald Feinberg, Ph.D., and Robert Shapiro, Ph.D.

FROM A "COMMONSENSE" VIEWPOINT, nothing seems easier than to tell what is alive and what is not. Humans, birds, plants, and even bacteria look and act very differently from rocks, sand, and other nonliving things on Earth.

The difference was underlined in a very funny way a few years ago when Pet Rocks were offered for sale in a number of stores. Pet Rocks were excellent at obeying certain familiar dog commands, such as "Sit" or "Stay." Getting them to "Come here" was naturally a bit harder to do.

While it is easy to describe the difference in behavior between a dog and a rock, it is surprisingly hard to capture the difference between the two in a precise definition. Especially when we try to extend our concepts and observations to less-familiar examples of Earth-life, we run into difficulties. A writer recently described the ocean floor as viewed by time-lapse photography:

"Something that for three months had looked like a rock got up and moved about a foot, then settled down again and looked like a rock for three more months. Another rocklike thing sprouted an arm and waved it about for 12 hours, then remained motionless for the rest of the six months."

For another example that is difficult to define, let us consider the tardigrade, a barely visible insect-like animal. Tardigrades can be dried out and stored in a bottle on a shelf for many years, to all intents like the lifeless ashes of Great-uncle Lemuel. But add water to instant tardigrade, and the animals will be restored to their normal state and scamper merrily about, no worse for their long, dry nap.

Is tardigrade powder alive? It is

BLACK UHURU

PROMOTIONAL COPY ONLY
NOT FOR SALE
STEREO
PRO 407-B
℗ 1983 Island Records, Inc.

WHAT IS LIFE? – 6:40
(D. Simpson)
Produced by BLACK UHURU,
STEVEN STANLEY & PAUL "GROUCHO" SMYKLE
Mixed by FRANCOIS KEVORKIAN &
PAUL "GROUCHO" SMYKLE
Ackee Music Inc.(ASCAP)

4TH & B'WAY™, A DIVISION OF ISLAND TRADING CO., 14 EAST 4TH STREET, NEW YORK, N.Y. 10012

NATURE VOL. 317 26 SEPTEMBER 1985

CORRESPONDENCE

281

The AIDS panic

SIR—Public pressure for protective measures against acquired immune deficiency syndrome (AIDS) is only now starting to surface[1]. Perhaps the greatest danger now is that the dramatic change in public attitudes towards the disease will have consequences more devastating than the syndrome itself. Growing demands for protection will force governments to adopt measures which, to be effective, may undermine the foundations of Western society, to the extent that they lead to segregation of the infected population, not only blood donors[2]. The US army has already made a pioneering decision in that direction[3].

A computerized listing of all seropositives used as a new basis for discrimination and eventual segregation of the potential viral carriers is not a fictitious danger. It is the logical outcome of the development of a fear for which the AIDS virus is less responsible than scientists and journalists. After accusing the sexual minority, rejected since biblical times by the prevalent religions, the authors of the sensational will now stress the number of victims[4] and emphasize the hope for a vaccine (R. Gallo quoted in *Le Monde*), while the scientists, having exhausted the immunosuppressive properties of sperm, seminal fluid and homosexuality, now predict the danger of a lethal pandemic within the next 15–25 years[5], forgetting that African AIDS, although appearing in 1970, has not fulfilled even part of the prophecy. The reasoning has been so simple as to appear flawless, as is always the danger with inductive science. A mere extrapolation from preliminary epidemiological data or other animal lentiviral diseases is sufficient to predict a pandemic in the 21st century, in the same simplistic way that for two years homosexuality was believed to be the cause of the syndrome, since AIDS was predominant in the homosexual population. The infectious agent hypothesis was then considered to be "too simplistic"[7].

There is no way out of this potentially explosive situation other than factual information. It is thus urgent to refrain from formulating too easy extrapolations, if we do not wish to spend the next twenty years with the fear of contamination. Establishing the time lapse during which seropositive individuals are viral carriers is under these circumstances a research priority second only to that aiming at the investigation of the mechanisms of resistance of those who, although infected with the virus, do not develop the full-blown disease.

However, perhaps the first priority is to inform the lay public so that the fear of the unknown does not develop into hysteria, and instead of promising vaccines, which we do not yet know how to produce, it is urgent to explain what AIDS *is not* and, by extrapolating from the known, define the limits of the epidemic rather than the boundaries of terror in our imagination.

DIMITRI VIZA

Faculté de Médecine,
Laboratoire d'Immunobiologie,
15, rue de l'Ecole de Médecine,
75006 Paris, France

1. *Nature* 316, 663–664 (1985).
2. Siegal, F.P. & Siegal, M. (eds) *AIDS: The Medical Mystery* (Group Press, New York, 1983).
3. *Nature* 316, 668 (1985).
4. *Le Monde*, 31 August (1985).
5. *Le Monde*, 17 July (1985).
6. Seale, J. *New Scientist* No. 1467, 29–30 (1985).
7. Sonnabend, J.A., Witkin, S.S. & Purtillo, D.T. in *The Acquired Immune Deficiency Syndrome and Infections of Homosexual Men* (eds Pearl, M.A. & Armstrong, D.) 409–425 (Yorke, New York, 1984).

What is life?

SIR—R.L. Hoult (*Nature* 316, 480; 1985) is brave to make a stab at clarifying what is meant by saying that a human embryo is "alive".

However, his attempt at distinguishing between dependent and independent viability — with embryos being dependently viable — is not very useful since the word viable means "capable of living either dependently or independently". Hence the problem of defining the words "alive" or "capable of living" is still not addressed in his letter.

The fundamentalists who seek to prevent embryo experimentation may not be impressed, in any case, by a distinction between dependent and independent viability.

The real need is for biologists to seek to change the terms of the debate on experimentation. The problem is that the argument that "embryos are not alive — in some sense or other" is purely defensive. And it is liable to be dismissed for seeking to blind the public with science.

At the root of the debate is a very serious question: "At what point should biologists and others stop seeking to improve the human condition?" Society has views and concerns about this question, as do biologists.

There is probably, for example, general concern that embryo experiments should stop at the point where there are feelings of pain in the embryo. That concern can only be addressed by biologists explaining vigorously and clearly what those words mean and what are the limits of current knowledge on pain in an embryo.

Since the fundamentalism of Darwin's days, the consensus view of society has shifted. Further shifts are likely if biologists are successful in explaining fully and clearly what they are up to, if they demonstrate honestly how their work seeks to improve the human condition and if they win the resources needed to do that job of explaining.

M.A.R. YUILLE

3a Halesworth Road,
London SE13 7TJ, UK

Good news for Spanish scientists

SIR—Alfonso Martínez Arias's recent letter (*Nature* 18 July, p.184) casts very serious doubts on the attitudes of the Spanish government to reincorporation into the scientific community of young scientists working abroad. I should like to report on recent steps that show, in my view, a much more serious commitment by our government than that conveyed by the statement of your correspondent on "national propaganda (words and wishes)".

First, special fellowships (of which 105 were awarded in August) have been created to help to reabsorb into the Spanish scientific community young researchers who have been working abroad. PhD degrees from foreign institutions are now automatically accepted.

Second, a programme was launched in 1984 to provide funding for both foreign and Spanish scientists intending to spend their sabbatical leave in Spain. Particularly in the case of Spaniards, this may lead to more permanent employment.

Third, in a recent programme for promoting young Spanish scientists to posts in universities and national research laboratories, credit has been given for time spent in foreign institutions. Last but not least, the present government's Law of University Reform has abolished, as a method of university recruitment, those peculiar endurance tests ("oposiciones") that brought so much misery and retardation to Spanish science.

Bureaucracy is, however, always present. Even if some of the statements by Alfonso Martínez Arias about PhD validation are grossly exaggerated, there is undoubtedly ample room for improvement. We are currently working on eliminating obstacles on the basis of the Law of University Reform.

Whether the actions I describe will break all the barriers above the Pyrenees I do not know. These mountains look at times frightfully high. Let us hope, at least, that we shall succeed in tunnelling through them.

J. M. ROJO

Secretary of State for Universities
and Research,
Serrano, 150, 28006 Madrid, Spain

Three of a kind

SIR—You refer to the University of New South Wales as "Sydney's other university" (*Nature* 316, 196; 1985). Actually there are three universities in Sydney. The University of Sydney provides a third option for students, and some very creditable research still goes on there.

MARK WESTOBY

School of Biological Sciences,
Macquarie University,
North Ryde, NSW 2113, Australia

WHAT IS LIFE ? LIFE AS A BIOINFORMATION SYSTEM

R.Lahoz-Beltrá
Cátedra de Biología Matemática,Facultad Ciencias Biológicas,
Universidad Complutense.Madrid 28040.Spain.

The aim of the present work is to apply the Shannon-Weaver (1949) theory of the information to the relation between the number of the nitrogen bases and the number of amino acids present in each one of the coacervates of the prebiotic soup (Oparin,1938).

In agreement with the information theory,the identification of a particular amino acid among m different amino acids will require a quantity of information equal to $I_m =$ $= \log_2 m$,whereas the quantity of information supplied by a nitrogen base in a system of n bases will be given by $I_n = \log_2 n$.

The proposed model is based on the following postulates:

i) The relation number of nitrogen bases/number of amino acids contained in each coacervate,will depend on which area of the soup are isolated such molecules by membrane formation.

ii) Not all nitrogen bases take part in the identification of an amino acid.However,from the total of these bases depend the total of amino acids among which one is going be identied.

iii) The number of amino acids takes a maximum value when $I_n = I_m$ or $\sum I_n = I_m$,whereas this does not take place it will fulfilled that $I_n > I_m$.

iv) We do not consider the repetition of bases of the same nature,for example AA,BBB,AAB, etc.Nevertheless,we permit the formation of groups of nitrogen bases (two bases codon, three bases codon,etc) of different nature,for example AB,ABC,etc.This will allows a greater simplicity of the model.

A system of these characteristics will be a BIOINFORMATION SYSTEM,in which the relation number of nitrogen bases/number of amino acids can be expressed as ( )$\underline{k}$(—( ).

In the parenthesis of the left the nitrogen bases,which participate in the identification of amino acids,are written,being k the total number of bases and it is omitted when k=1.In the parenthesis of the right we place the number of amino acids among which one of them is going to be identified,and whose number depend on the total number of bases of the system.As an example,a present-day organism will have the following expression:

$$(ABC)\underline{^{4}}(-(abc..20)$$

Since from the number of the nitrogen bases present is going to depend – – – – – the number of amino acids able to support the system in agreement with the theory of the information,in the proposed model we have analysed the bioinformation systems constituted by 1,2,3 or 4 nitrogen bases.Once analyzed,these have been clasified into three groups according to the loss of information which takes place when a base or group of them

PERSPECTIVES

WHAT IS LIFE?

. . . .

FROM QUANTUM FLUX TO THE SELF

ERNEST LAWRENCE ROSSI

There is a destination, a possible goal. That is the way of individuation. Individuation means becoming an "individual," and, in so far as "individuality" embraces our innermost, last, and incomparable uniqueness, it also implies becoming one's own self. We could therefore translate individuation as "coming to selfhood" or "self-realization." (p. 173)

The transcendent function does not proceed without aim and purpose, but leads to the revelation of the essential man. It is in the first place a purely natural process, which may in some cases pursue its course without the knowledge or assistance of the individual, and can sometimes forcibly accomplish itself in the face of opposition. The meaning and purpose of the process is the realization, in all its aspects, of the personality originally hidden away in the embryonic germ-plasm; the production and unfolding of the original, potential wholeness.

C. G. Jung, *Two Essays on Analytical Psychology,*
(Vol. 7), *Collected Works*

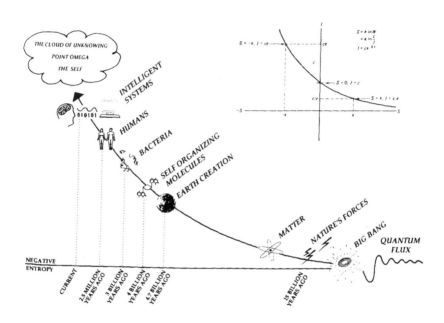

FIGURE 1: *The evolution of the universe from the Big Bang to the Self. This illustration was adapted from Tom Stonier's mathematical formulation (diagrammed in the upper right)* in Information and the Internal Structure of the Universe.[1]

International Society History Philosophy Social Studies for Biology
July 1993 - Brandeis University - session on Define LIFE : **WHAT IS LIFE?**
Organized by CG Winder - UWO Geology, London CANADA -N6A 5B7

DEFINITIONS OF LIFE - Selected from the published literature (not exhaustive)
****

DICTIONARIES
.........\#\#\#\#\#\#\#\#\#\#\#\#\#.....

FUNK & WAGNELL STANDARD COLLEGE DICTIONARY
The form of existence that distinguishes plants and animals from inorganic substances
and dead organisms, characterized by the properties and functions of protoplasmas
manifested in metabolism, growth, reproduction, irritability, and internally initiated
adaptions of individual organisms to the environment. ...

RANDOM HOUSE DICTIONARY OF THE ENGLISH LANGUAGE
The condition that distinguishes animals and plants from inorganic objects and dead
organisms, being manifest by growth through metabolism, reproduction, and powerof
adaption to environment through changes originating internally.

Webster's New World Dictionary, College Edition.
That property of plants and animals which makes it possible for them to take in food,
get energy from it, grow, adapt to their surroundings, and reproduce their kind; it
is the quality that distinguishes a living animal or plant from inorganic matter or
dead organisms.

Webster's New Lexicon, 1987.
The state of an organism characterized by certain processes and ability that include
metabolism, growth, reproduction, and response.

PUBLISHED BY INDIVIDUALS
\#

ISAAC ASIMOV, Life and Time, 1978, p.7 & 9 (compiled)
LIFE is the property of objects composed of cells with active DNA and/or RNA, which
can, actually or potentially, in whole or in part, move independently, sense, respond
adaptively, metabolize, grow, and reproduce so, as to decrease its entropy. (A virus
has DNA).

J.D.BERNAL,1951, in Lovelock, 1988, p.25
Life is one member of the class of phenomena which are open or continuous reaction
systems able to decrease their internal entropy at the expense of free energy taken
from the environment and subsequently rejected in degraded form.

TIM M. BERRA, Evolution etc., Stanford Press, 1990, p.75.
Living things metabolize, reproduce, respond to stimuli and adapt. Viruses are on the
borderline between life and non-life. A single cell seems to be the smallest unit
that can be said to be alive.

JIM BROOKS, 'Origins of Life', Lyons Publishing, 1985, p. 81.
A system that everyone would presumably accept as living can be defined as a
metabolizing system that reproduces itself, mutates, and reproduces mutations.
Wherever living things exist, they are likely to be carbon based, dependent on a
supply of liquid water and contingent on either the absence of more than minute
quantities of free oxygen or the presence of suitable oxygen-mediating enzyme
systems.
Life is the structure-replication of enzymes ensured by exactly-reproduced nucleic
acid molecules.
Life has the capacity of self-repair.

I.L. COHEN, New Res. Publ.,1984,p.31-32   (compiled)
The cell, including bacteria, viruses, and amoeba, the basic building block of life,
performing all the functions, to sustain its own form, will nourish, digest, eject
excreta, breathe and reproduce, is an independent complete life-machine. --- the cell
is a complex chemical factory with hundreds of actions and reactions.

P.W. DAVIS & E.P. SOLOMON, The World of Biology, 1978
A living system is able to move, grow, respond, carry on self-regulating metablosim,
adapt, and reproduce. Order is the hallmark of LIFE.

DITFURTH, H.v., The Origins of Life, Harper & Row, 1982, p.23.
There are --- life functions so elementary that their presence can be demonstrated in
all living creatures -- (including) -- the metabolic functions required for
assimilation and conversion of energy. A living being that does not engage in a
continual exchange of energy with its environment is simply unthinkable.

THEODOSIUS DOBZHANSKY in 'MANKIND EVOLVING', 1961, P.41.
Life is unceasing development, although some organisms, such as seeds and spores of
plants, may remain quiescent for more or less long periods of time.

C.E. Folsome, "The origins of life", Freeman, p.73, 1979.
Life is that property of matter that results in the coupled cycling of bioelements in
aqueous solutions,-ultimately driven by radiant energy to attain maximum complexity.
....
J.B.S. HALDANE, 'What is Life?', p.56, 1947
"I am not going to answer this question. ---- Life is a pattern of chemical
processes."
....
JIM HARTING -- OASIS NEWSLETTER   v.4.2,#12,summer 1991
Life is the ability to temporarily defeat the Second Law of Thermodynamics(entropy)
by coupling the energy requirements of anabolic reaction to the energy release of
catabolic reactions, using enzymes that are the blue-print in the changeable genetic
code, DNA.
....
JAMES LOVELOCK, Gaia, 1979, p.152
A common state of matter found at Earth's surface and throughout the oceans. It is
composed of intricate combinations of the common elements hydrogen, carbon, oxygen,
nitrogen, sulphur, and phosphorous with many other elements in trace amounts. Most
forms of life can instantly be recognized without prior experience and are frequently
edible. The state of life, however, has so far resisted all attempts at a formal
physical definition.
....
JAMES LOVELOCK,The Ages of GAIA, 1988, p.27.
Life is a self organizing system, contained within boundaries, characterized by an
actively sustained low entropy.
....
PETER MOLTON, J. Brit. Interplanet., 1978
Life is defined as regions of order which use energy to maintain their organization
against the disruptive force of entropy.
....
E.G. NISBET, Living Earth, 1991, p.31 & 33
All LIFE shares the property of increasing local order by making the environment
around it more chaotic. --- The cell is the basic building block of LIFE.
....
RAYMOND J. NOGAR in THE WISDOM OF EVOLUTION, Mentor,1963, p.110.
LIFE is the result of protoplasmic activity [living matter], the properties [unique
characteristics] of which are: cellular organization,chemical composition, metabolism
involving the powers of maintenance,growth, repair, and reproduction,and irritability
resulting in the power of adaption.
LIFE, to the biologist, denotes the totality of self-reproducing metabolic
organizations of matter and energy comprised under the head of "organisms".
A living thing is an organism or organized unity showing the activities of
maintenance, development and reproduction directed by the vital process to the end of
completion of normal life-cycle. It is directive activity shown by individual
organisms that distinguish living things from inanimate objects.
....
F.H.T. RHODES, 'The Evolution of Life', Penguin, 1959,[abstracted]
Life is a series of processes which take place within certain levels of organization
of matter. The processes include growth, movement, reproduction, metabolism,
irritability, and so on. The basic 'stuff' of living organisms is 'protoplasm',
consisting of a complex mixture of water, various organic compounds (proteins,
nucleic acids, fats, and carbohydrates, etc.) and a number of salts (sodium chloride,
calcium carbonate, etc.).
....
J.H. RUSH, The Dawn of Life, 1957.
The chemical characteristics of living organisms (include) re-activity, lability,
reproducibility, and complexity. Living systems are highly reactive, carry on
chemical transformations at rates thousands or millions of times faster than the
rates of most non-living mixtures of organic compounds. Living material is
chemically labile, and maintains a sensitive state of equilibrium, so reactions occur
in reponse to very small scale changes in temperature, concentrations or other
environmental factors. Living systems are highly complex, composed of hydrogen,
carbon, nitrogen, oxygen, sodium, magnesium, phosphorus, sulphur, chlorine,
potassium, calcium and iron. Carbon is the key element in combination with hydrogen,
oxygen, nitrogen, phosphorus, and sulphur.
....
ERWIN SCHRODINGER, What is life? -- abstracted from Lovelock, 1988
Life is the amazing property and characteristic ability to move upstream against the
flow of time, a paradoxical contradiction of the second law which states that
everything is, always has been and will always run down to equilibrium and death;
life evolved to even greater complexity; an unstable state which has persisted on
Earth for a sizable fraction of the age of the universe.
....
JOHN MAYNARD SMITH, Problems of Biology, Oxford, 1986
The forms of living organisms remain constant but their composition is constantly
changing with metabolism; parts of the organism have functions, which contribute to
the survival and reproduction of the whole. Entities with the properities of
multiplication, variation, and heredity are alive, those lacking one or more of these
properties are not.
....

Sitting alongside Evelyn Fox Keller in 2015 in an MIT storeroom as she looks through metal filing cabinets holding a fragmentary archive of her professional life, we join her in searching for a file entitled "What Is Life?" The papers in these cabinets date back to the 1950s, when she began studying physics; through the 1960s, when she became interested in molecular and mathematical biology; into the 1970s, when she started writing on gender and science; through the 1980s, when the matter of language and science captured her attention; and into the last two decades, during which time she returned to conceptual questions in biology. We happen upon a folder labeled "What Is Life?," which appears to be for a first-year undergraduate course of the same title that Evelyn taught. We find a photocopy of a collection of definitions of life she gathered in preparation for a panel convened by geologist C. Gordon Winder of the University of Western Ontario at the 1993 meetings of the International Society for the History, Philosophy, and Social Studies of Biology. There's a file named "Life," another just called "Life/Death." One uncategorized folder contains a piece by Ursula K. Le Guin. Another includes a list of eighty-four guests to invite to a party. Lynn Margulis is on the roster. Evelyn finds the paper we were looking for. It is a manuscript of a talk she gave in 2007 when she held the Blaise Pascal Research Chair, awarded by the Préfecture de la région d'Île-de-France.

Sophia Roosth and Stefan Helmreich

apathy

reconfigure

Once Again, "What Is Life?"

"What is life?" is surely one of the most curious questions in the history of biology. It is curious in a number of ways, one of which is that, while it would certainly seem to be a foundational question, it has had a surprisingly minor place in the history of the life sciences—at least once biology came to be accepted as a scientific discipline in its own right. For the most part, it has been regarded as superfluous to serious scientific study of the living world. Indeed, for long periods, and in many areas of the life sciences, the question was considered pointless, if not altogether meaningless: As N.W. Pirie wrote in his 1937 diatribe, "nothing turns on whether a virus is described as a living organism or not."[1] Put simply, once they could inhabit a domain of their own, biologists found themselves happily unencumbered by the absence of a definition of the term "living" in their actual practices of investigating vital phenomena.

In fact, over the past half century, the question has most commonly been associated with the name of a physicist and not a biologist, for it was the title of Erwin Schrödinger's famous essay, published in 1944.[2] Schrödinger's choice of title was undoubtedly regarded with suspicion by many biologists, but his own status—together, of course, with the dramatic successes of molecular biology—worked ultimately to mollify that distrust. Still, Schrödinger did not exactly provide an answer to the question. What he did offer was a proposal the significance of which accrued only in hindsight: He proposed that the chromosome fiber—in his view, the most essential feature of the living organism—was an "aperiodic crystal" containing a "code-script" that specified both the form and construction of the organism. Ten years later, James Watson and Francis Crick's elucidation of the structure of DNA was widely taken to vindicate Schrödinger. His essay now found a ready and growing audience among biologists, and indeed, came to be read as having signaled the arrival of an unexpectedly simple answer to what many had previously regarded as an

1   N.W. Pirie, "The Meaninglessness of the Terms Life and Living," in J. Needham and D. E. Green (eds), *Perspectives in Biochemistry*. Cambridge: Cambridge University Press, 1937, pp. 11–22, here p. 22.
2   Erwin Schrödinger, *What Is Life? The Physical Aspect of the Living Cell*. Cambridge: Cambridge University Press, 1944.

impossible question. Molecular biology may not have provided a definition of "life" which would satisfy everyone, but the two-fold discovery that (a) genes were made up of DNA, and (b) the structure of DNA provided a mechanism for "self-replication" did seem to provide a simple criterion for distinguishing the "living" from the "non-living." What is life? It is in its essence a code-script realized in long sequences of DNA nucleotides. Or so it seemed. Here was an answer that seemed to lay the question to rest. For a while.

Schrödinger was, of course, not the first to ask what life is. But what neither he nor his predecessors did ask is, what kind of a question were they posing? Or, to put it differently, what kind of an answer would have qualified? Often, when people ask if something is alive, the object at issue is already assumed to belong to the biological realm. And the question they are asking is a diachronic one: Is the object (now, organism) in question either still or yet alive? Has its life ended? Has it begun? But for Schrödinger, the question of "What is life?" is of a different kind, synchronic rather than diachronic. How is this object to be taxonomically classified? Is it to be grouped with the living or with the non-living? Also, Schrödinger did not notice—any more than others did who had earlier so inquired—the extent to which their own posing of the question rests on a particular presupposition, namely that a unifying (or modal) essence underlying all living forms not only exists, but also can be identified. In other words, their question presupposed that there is such a thing as life itself that can be defined (or, to put it differently, that "life" is what philosophers call a "natural kind"). Indeed, their query makes no sense without such a presupposition.

Moreover, their query already recognizes some sort of category to which the term "life" already refers. Its aim is to clarify, to make more precise, a concept or notion already at hand. But not any kind of notion will do. François Jacob modifies Michel Foucault's infamous claim that, in the eighteenth century, "life itself did not exist"[3] by suggesting instead that it was "The concept of life [that] did not exist"[4]

3　Michel Foucault, *Les mots et les choses: Une archéologie des sciences humaines*. Paris: Éditions Gallimard, 1966; trans. Alan Sheridan, *The Order of Things: An Archaeology of the Human Sciences*. New York: Pantheon Books, 1970, pp. 127–28.

4　François Jacob, *La logique du vivant: une histoire de l'hérédité*. Paris: Gallimard, 1970; trans. Betty E Spillmann, *The Logic of Life: A History of Heredity*, 2nd ed. New York: Pantheon, 1976, p. 89.

prior to the nineteenth century. He writes that his claim is "shown by the definition in the *Grande Encyclopédie*, an almost self-evident truth: life 'is the opposite of death.'"[5] Jacob explains his dissatisfaction with such earlier definitions by saying they do not provide us with a positive characterization of "the properties of living organisms"; they do not tell us what life is. But what exactly does he mean by this? Is it that Denis Diderot's definition is "self-evident," that it is negative (i.e. based on "opposition") and not positive, or just that it invokes the wrong contrast class (i.e. "death")? Or is it all of the above? Some indication of what prevents Diderot's (and, of course, Xavier Bichat's) notion of "life" from being a "concept" in Jacob's view can be gleaned from the contrast with which he continues: "At the beginning of the nineteenth century, on the other hand, what mattered was to define the properties of living organisms." But what might a focus on "properties" have meant to the authors who first marked the distinction, and why is it now claimed, by both Jacob and Foucault, to have been so critical?

To help answer this question, and to clarify the point I want to make, let me turn to Jean-Baptiste Lamarck. Like Jacob, Lamarck begins with a contrast, an example of how not to proceed. He writes:

> Life, said M. Richerand, is a collection of phenomena which succeed one another for a limited period in organised bodies.
> He should have said, life is a phenomenon which gives rise to a collection of other phenomena, etc.; for it is not these other phenomena that constitute life, but they are themselves caused by life. A study of the phenomena resulting from the existence of life in a body provides no definition of life, and shows nothing more than objects that life itself has produced.[6]

The notion of "life" which "provides no definition," and against which Lamarck juxtaposes his own efforts, is merely an ostensive (or extensive) one—only pointing to a collection of phenomena that exhibit the property in question without providing any prior specification of the

5 Ibid.
6 Jean-Baptiste Lamarck, *Philosophie zoologique; ou Exposition des considérations relatives à l'histoire naturelle des animaux*. Paris: Dentu, 1809; trans. Hugh Elliot, *Zoological Philosophy: An Exposition with Regard to the Natural History of Animals*. London: Macmillan, 1914, p. 201.

limits to or the boundary of that collection. What Lamarck is after is a constitutive definition: He seeks a characterization of the common denominator underlying (and "causing") the phenomena in Richerand's collection, a characterization which will clearly mark the limits of that collection. At the same time, he argues that such an effort requires a new demarcation of "living bodies," contrasted not—as Diderot and Bichat would have it—to "dead" bodies, but to "inorganic" ones. He wrote:

> Yet if we wish to arrive at a real knowledge of what constitutes life, what it consists of, what are the causes and laws which control so wonderful a natural phenomenon, and how life itself can originate those numerous and astonishing phenomena exhibited by living bodies, we must above all pay very close attention to the differences existing between inorganic and living bodies; and for this purpose a comparison must be made between the essential characters of these two kinds of bodies.[7]

Lamarck's move in this passage is two-fold: on the one hand, from an ostensive to constitutive (or from extensive to intensive) definition, and on the other hand, contrasting "life" not to death but to the "inorganic." But it is precisely the latter, that is, attention to the "extreme difference" between the living and the non-living, which by Lamarck's reasoning, makes the former possible. It is this distinction between living and non-living that permits "a real knowledge of what constitutes life"—or, to use Jacob's term, which permits positive characterization of "the properties of living organisms." Jacob is no Lamarckian, but nonetheless, Lamarck's composite move clearly illustrates the shift that Jacob (like Foucault) claims as transformative for the biological sciences. It elevates earlier notions of "life" to that of a "concept," to an abstraction of essences on the basis of which the world of the living can be set apart as a unitary entity with its own distinguishing "properties."

Foucault has emphasized the taxonomic dimensions of this shift: the emergence of a new way of classifying natural objects that divided the "living" (plants and animals) from the "non-living"

7   Ibid., 191.

(minerals). And certainly, it was crucial for the demarcation of a distinctive science of biology. But perhaps its greatest significance (at least for the life sciences) is to be seen not so much in the articulation of a new systematics (and even less in the rise of "a notion like that of life"),[8] but rather in the conception of "life" as a natural kind. By this, I mean the notion of "life" as the fundamental essence or set of properties common to all the beings we call "living" and absent from those we call "non-living." Living beings are not themselves instances of "life" but only its manifestations: They are "caused by life." If the question of "What is life?" did not make sense prior to the nineteenth century, it is not because life did not exist, but rather, because in earlier times, life was not a natural kind. To be sure, Lamarck's characterization of the kind of entity life is depends (just as does Jacob's, just as does Schrödinger's, or indeed, just as does any attempt at such a characterization) on a particular taxonomy. But it is worth noting that, while such a formulation may have been facilitated by the new systematics, it was not logically dependent upon it—any demarcation could, in principle, have served.

Today, the question of "What is life?" comes to the fore once again with the appearance of new kinds of entities claiming the status of living. These entities invite the formation of new groupings—ones that necessarily violate older taxonomies. Instead of linking together into a single category of plants and animals, they might conjoin chemical blobs, macro-molecules, genetic algorithms, and robots together with life as we know it; or they might also include, as Charles Bennett once suggested, thunderstorms and umbrellas; or, as the early cyberneticists claimed, armies and vending machines.[9]

How we answer these questions depends, as it always has, on where we draw the boundary of "life." And that is a human decision. It depends on our local needs and interests, on our estimates of the costs and benefits of doing so, and also, of course, on our larger cultural and historical location. The notion of including at least some

8   Michel Foucault in Arnold Davidson (ed.), *Foucault and His Interlocutors.* Chicago, IL: University of Chicago Press, 1997, p. 110.
9   Charles H. Bennett, "On the Nature and Origin of Complexity in Discrete, Homogeneous, Locally-Interacting Systems," *Foundations of Physics*, vol. 16, no. 6 (1986), pp. 585-92.

of these entities would have seemed absurd to people living not so long ago—indeed, it seems absurd to me now. But that does not mean that we will not, or even that we should not, do so. It only means that the question "What is life?" is a historical question, answerable only in terms of the categories by which we as human actors choose to abide, the differences that we as human actors choose to honor, and not in either logical, scientific, or technical terms. It is in this sense that I argue for the category of life as a kind of family, a family that is humanly rather than naturally delineated.

What is Artificial Life?

A snappy answer [Langton, 1989]:

> The study of man-made systems that exhibit behaviors characteristic
> of natural living systems.

[Langton, 1992]:

> Artificial Life is a field of study devoted to understanding life by
> attempting to abstract the fundamental dynamical principles underlying
> biological phenomena, and recreating these dynamics in other physical
> media- such as computers- making them accessible to new kinds of
> experimental manipulation and testing.
> ...
> In addition to providing new ways to study the biological phenomena
> associated with life here on Earth, *life-as-we-know-it*,
> Artificial Life allows us to extend our studies to the larger domain
> of "bio-logic" of possible life, *life-as-it-could-be* ...

[Langton, 1994]:

> Among all of the things that artificial life is or will come to be,
> however, it is probably safe to say that the field as a whole
> represents an attempt to vastly increase the role of synthesis in
> the study of biological phenomena.

[Ray, 1994]:

> Artificial Life (AL) is the enterprise of understanding biology by
> constructing biological phenomena out of artificial components, rather
> than breaking natural life forms down into their component parts. It is
> the synthetic rather than the reductionist approach.

[Taylor et al., 1994]:

> ... Artificial Life models ...   are powerful enough to capture much of
> the complexity of living systems, yet in a form that is more easily

'What is life?' as
a problem in history

STEPHEN JAY GOULD

Museum of Comparative Zoology, Harvard University, Cambridge, Massachusetts

WHAT IS LIFE? AS A MODERNIST MANIFESTO

The obviously true may be devilishly difficult to define – as best exemplified
by Louis Armstrong's famous retort to a naively passionate fan's request for
a definition of jazz: 'Man, if you gotta ask you'll never know.' It is similarly
undeniable that Erwin Schrödinger's *What is Life?* ranks among the most
important books in 20th century biology, but the reasons for its great influence
seem oddly elusive. Brevity may be the soul of wit (as garrulous old Polonius
told us), and short works are rare blessings in a profession that too often judges
worth by literal ponderousness. But *What is Life?*, in its ninety pages, seems a
bit too spare and too elliptical to carry such intellectual weight (though, in a
ruthlessly practical sense, such brevity may define the essential differences
between attention and oblivion in a profession dominated by doers rather than
readers). For example, I think we may be confident of the correct, if necessarily
conjectural answer to an old puzzle in 'iffy' history: how would the history
of science have differed if Wallace had never lived and Darwin had thereby
acquired the leisure to write the many-volumed work he intended, rather than
the hurried 'abstract' known as the *Origin of Species?* The answer – since the
intellectual world was clearly poised to accept evolution – must be: none what-
soever, except that Darwin would have had the same impact with many, many
fewer people having read the book. Moreover, much of *What is Life?*'s intellectual foundation – Delbrück's early ideas on reasons for the gene's stability –
turn out to be quite wrong (see Crow, 1992, p. 238). Why, then, are we so
rightly celebrating this semicentenary?

First of all, the testimony of seminal importance by so many of the founders
of modern molecular biology cannot be gainsaid. Jim Watson credits

[25]

LYNN MARGULIS
DORION SAGAN

WHAT IS LIFE?

FOREWORD BY
NILES ELDREDGE

So, what is life?

Life is evolutionary exuberance; it is what happens when expanding populations of sensing, active organisms knock up against each other and work things out. Life is animals at play. It is a marvel of inventions for cooling and warming, collecting and dispersing, eating and evading, wooing and

So, what is life?

Life is the transmutation of sunlight. It is the energy and matter of the sun become the green fire of photosynthesizing beings. It is the natural seductiveness of flowers. It is the warmth of the

So, what is life?

It is a material process, sifting and surfing over matter like a strange, slow wave. It is a controlled, artistic chaos, a set of chemical reactions so staggeringly complex that more than eighty million years ago it produced the mammalian brain that now, in human form, composes love letters and uses

So, what is life?

Life is planetary exuberance, a solar phenomenon. It is the astronomically local transmutation of Earth's air, water, and sun into cells. It is an intricate pattern of growth and death, dispatch and retrench-ment, transformation and decay. Life is the single

So, what is life?

Life is a network of cross-kingdom alliances, of which Kingdom Mychota is a willing and crafty participant. Life is an orgy of attractions, from the trickery of counterfeit "flowers" to the strange allures of truffle and difficult-to-swallow hallucino-gens. As fungi, life seeks out the underworld of soil

So, what is life?

Life is the representation, the "presencing" of past chemistries, a past environment of the early Earth that, because of life, remains on the modern Earth. It is the watery, membrane-bound encapsulation of

Arnold De Loof

Wat is leven ?

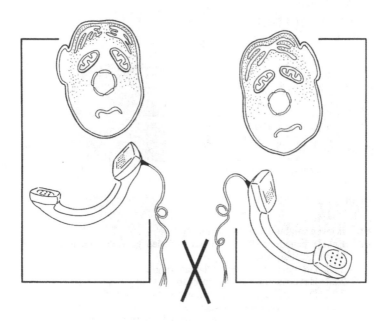

Dood: het irreversibel verlies van het vermogen tot communicatie op het hoogste niveau van compartimentele organisatie.

What is Life?

THE ORIGINALITY, IRREDUCIBILITY, AND VALUE OF LIFE

Josef Seifert

51

Two

WHAT IS BIOLOGICAL LIFE?
THE IRREDUCIBILITY OF VEGETATIVE LIFE
(*BIOS*) TO ORDERED AND CHAOTIC
PHYSICAL SYSTEMS

1. Irreducibility and Undefinability of Organic Life, yet Possibility of Its Essential Definition through Its Various Marks

What, then, is organic life? I am using here the terms "*bios*," "biological life," "vegetative life," and "organic life" as synonyms which indicate the kind of life which we find in all living entities on earth, including plants. The term "sensitive life" refers to animals (and human beings), "mental or rational life" to persons only.

Bios is an astonishing phenomenon. Like all absolutely original and ultimate data, for example, being, *bios* defies our attempts to define it. We realize that all the complex protein, nucleotide-structures, and the most diverse phenomena linked to life, as, for example, genetic codes, cannot explain what life itself is though it presupposes or originates these or similar phenomena. Apart from life (proteins in an organism at the moment of its death or genetic codes stored on a computer), all these elements would be part of a dead thing and not constitute life.

Max Scheler calls life a "genuine essence" (*eine echte Wesenheit*), a "fundamental phenomenon" (*ein Grundphänomen*), an "underivable arch-phenomenon" (*ein unableitbares Urphänomen*), in order to point at this irreducible and original identity of life with respect to which all forms of reductionism must fail.[1] Following some authors, we can render in the following "*Urphänomen*" also as "*Urphenomenon*" (instead of arch-phenomenon). Viktor Frankl, in his "Der Mensch auf der Suche nach Sinn: Anthropologische Grundlagen der Psychotherapie," gives a striking example of a reductionism, which he calls, jokingly, "oxidationism." His teacher of biology explained that life is nothing but processes of combustion or oxidation, a statement to which the young boy Frankl retorted: "But what then, professor, is the meaning of life?" Frankl observes convincingly that it might not be by chance that this teacher later became a fanatic Nazi because Nazism is based on a reductionistic and meaningless concept of life.[2]

In a sense, life allows us only to say what George Edward Moore said about the good: Life is life. Note the striking text of Moore:

Critical Reviews™ in Biomedical Engineering, 28(3&4):545–550 (2000)

What Is Life, and What Is a Machine? The Ontology of Bioengineering

Curtis R. Naser

Department of Philosophy, 315 Donnarumma Hall, Fairfield University, Fairfield, CT 06430

ABSTRACT: In his Keynote address to the First Conference at Clemson University on Ethical Issues in Biomedical Engineering, George Bugliarello suggested that a most important ethical issue for bioengineering "is the positioning of the bio-machine interface." "Where," he asked, "should the biological organism end and the machine begin?" Central to this question of the limits of life and engineering is the more fundamental question of how life differs and how it is similar to a machine. This paper argues that until very recently, science, by its very nature, has treated life *as if it were a machine*, or has treated the parts of living systems *as if they were machines*. The distinctive feature of a machine is that its behavior is linear and hence predictable. On the other hand, living organisms may not be linear, but rather nonlinear systems. Thus, the interface between organism and machine may be conceived as the interface between nonlinear and linear systems.

KEY WORDS: philosophy of biology, reductionism, holism, nonlinear systems.

In his Keynote address to the First Conference on Ethical Issues in Biomedical Engineering at Clemson University, George Bugliarello suggested that "[I]n terms of limits, a most important ethical issue for bioengineering is the positioning of the bio-machine interface."[1] This is not the typical sort of *ethical* question, since it does not directly ask 'What *ought* the engineer to do?' or, 'What *good* does bioengineering seek?' Rather, the question Dr. Bugliarello has asked pertains to *what* the thing *is*, which is the object of bioengineering.

Bioengineering has two distinct objects: the living organism (and perhaps even populations of organisms or whole ecosystems), and the machine. Machines per se typically do not entail any special ethical considerations. Indeed, there is no ethics of the machine, although there certainly are ethical considerations about the uses of machines. Living organisms are more properly the objects of ethical reflection, although there is debate over which types of organisms deserve ethical consideration. Few doubt that the rational animal is both the center of ethical reflection and its primary object, but there is some disagreement over whether the umbrella of ethical reflection should not extend to other species, and, if so, to what species; and beyond that, to ecosystems and the environment. At the risk of anthropocentrism, I will confine myself to the interface between human beings and machines, and individual human beings and machines at that.

HUMANITIES AND MEDICINE

What Is Life? Prerequisites for a Definition

Douglas E. Dix[a]

Department of Biology, University of Biology, West Hartford, Connecticut

Biologists view life as transient while theologians see it as eternal. An unbiased definition for life would respect both views until one or both were eliminated by evidence. This paper identifies prerequisites for such a definition. First among these is that all assumptions be made explicit. Currently "life" is surrounded by implicit assumptions, e.g., that it is what organisms lose at death or that it is eternal, that its quality is inversely related to personal distress, that it originated some four billion years ago, and that animate matter can be distinguished from inanimate matter. None of these assumptions are supported by data. It is possible therefore that "life" is as meaningless as phlogiston. If life has meaning, i.e., if it is true, it must be as permanent as buoyancy, gravity, electricity, and the other truths of nature. Any definition for life that would permit such truth to be seen must be free of unwarranted assumptions. For the moment, at least, such a definition would need to be loosely structured and broadly focused. It would need to describe the long and convoluted process by which matter and energy form organisms which then evolve to form conscious organisms which then explore nature and eventually discover truth. Such a definition would include all the reactions and interactions of matter and energy and all the aspects of conscious discovery. It would suffer from superficiality, but, by being free from bias, provide a foundation for dialogue between biologists and theologians.

INTRODUCTION AND METHOD

Life is common to the vocabulary of two divergent disciplines: biology with its focus on events before death, and theology with its focus on events after death. In biology, life is assumed to be transient, i.e., the antonym of death. In theology, life is assumed to be eternal. Which assumption is valid? What, precisely, is life? Schrodinger called attention to the need for definition, but never measured life, or even specified its units of measure [1]. Does life come in liters or grams or calories? Is the total amount of life fixed or variable, and, if variable, how does it vary over time and space, and from one organism to another, and across the different species? What amount of life presently exists on Earth? Is there a relationship between this amount and the state of the ecosystem, or the health of organisms, or the number or rate of births or deaths? These are the kinds of questions that students of life should expect to pursue in life science. But there are no answers and no reasonable approaches to finding any. The definition of life remains a problem with semantic as well as biological and theological implications [2-3].

From the biological perspective, life is nothing but biochemistry [1, 4-7], i.e., the "orderly and lawful behavior of matter"

[a]*To whom correspondence may be addressed:* Douglas E. Dix, Department of Biology, University of Hartford, West Hartford, CT 06117. Tel.: 860-768-4261 (O), 860-243-1116 (H); Fax: 860-768-5002; E-mail: dix@mail.hartford.edu.
[b]*Abbreviations:* ATP, Adenosine Triphosphate
Received: January 10, 2003; Returned for revisions February 27, 2003; Accepted July 12, 2003

Unsolved Mystery

What Is Life—and How Do We Search for It in Other Worlds?

Chris P. McKay

I need a "tricorder"—the convenient, hand-held device featured on *Star Trek* that can detect life forms even from orbit. Unfortunately, we don't have a clue how a tricorder might work, since life forms don't seem to have any observable property that distinguishes them from inanimate matter. Furthermore, we lack a definition of life that can guide a search for life outside Earth. How can we find what we can't define? An answer may lie in the observation that life uses a small, discrete set of organic molecules as basic building blocks. On the surface of Europa and in the subsurface of Mars, we can search for alien but analogous patterns in the organics.

Life As We Know It

The obvious diversity of life on Earth overlies a fundamental biochemical and genetic similarity. The three main polymers of biology—the nucleic acids, the proteins, and the polysaccharides— are built from 20 amino acids, five nucleotide bases, and a few sugars, respectively. Together with lipids and fatty acids, these are the main constituents of biomass: the hardware of life (Lehninger 1975, p 21). The DNA and RNA software of life is also common, indicating shared descent (Woese 1987). But with only one example of life—life on Earth—it is not all that surprising that we do not have a fundamental understanding of what life is. We don't know which features of Earth life are essential and which are just accidents of history.

Our lack of data is reflected in our attempts to define life. Koshland (2002) lists seven features of life: (1) program (DNA), (2) improvisation (response to environment), (3) compartmentalization, (4) energy, (5) regeneration, (6) adaptability, and (7) seclusion (chemical control and selectivity). A simpler definition is that life is a material system that undergoes reproduction, mutation, and natural selection (McKay 1991). Cleland and Chyba (2002) have suggested that life

might be like water, hard to define phenomenologically, but easy to define at the fundamental level. But life is like fire, not water—it is a process, not a pure substance. Such definitions are grist for philosophical discussion, but they neither inform biological research nor provide a basis for the search for life on other worlds.

The simplest, but not the only, proof of life is to find something that is alive. There are only two properties that can determine if an object is alive: metabolism and motion. (Metabolism is used here to include an organism's life functions, biomass increase, and reproduction.) All living things require some level of metabolism to remain viable against entropy. Movement (either microscopic or macroscopic) in response to stimuli or in the presence of food can be a convincing indicator of a living thing. But both metabolism (fire) and motion (wind) occur in nature in the absence of biology.

The practical approach to the search for life is to determine what life needs. The simplest list is probably: energy, carbon, liquid water, and a few other elements such as nitrogen, sulfur, and phosphorus (McKay 1991). Life requires energy to maintain itself against entropy, as does any self-organizing open system. In the memorable words of Erwin Schrödinger (1945), "It feeds on negative entropy." On Earth, the vast majority of life forms ultimately derive their energy from sunlight. The only other source of primary productivity known is chemical energy, and there are only two ecosystems known, both methanogen-based (Stevens and McKinley 1995; Chapelle et al. 2002), that rely exclusively on chemical energy (that is, they do not use sunlight or its product, oxygen). Photosynthetic organisms can use sunlight at levels below the level of sunlight at the orbit of Pluto (Ravens et al. 2000); therefore, energy is not the limitation for life. Carbon, nitrogen, sulfur, and phosphorus are the elements of life,

and they are abundant in the Solar System. Indeed, the Sun and the outer Solar System have more than 10,000 times the carbon content of the bulk of Earth (McKay 1991). When we scan the other worlds of our Solar System, the missing ecological ingredient for life is liquid water. It makes sense, then, that the search for liquid water is currently the first step in the search for life on other worlds. The presence of liquid water is a powerful indication that the ecological prerequisites for life are satisfied.

Orbital images, such as the canyon in Figure 1, show clear evidence of stable and repeated, if not persistent, flow of a low-viscosity fluid on Mars at certain times in its past history. The fluid was probably water, but the images could also suggest wind, ice, lava, even carbon dioxide or sulfur dioxide. Recently, results from the Mars Exploration Rover missions have shown that this liquid carried salts and precipitated hematite in concretions. The case for water, we could say, is tight.

On Jupiter's moon Europa, the cracks and icebergs on the surface of the ice indicate water beneath the ice, but not necessarily at the present time. Present water on Europa is indicated by the magnetic disturbance Europa makes as it moves through Jupiter's magnetic field, not unlike the way coins in the pocket of a passenger will set off an airport metal detector. Europa has a large conductor, and this is most likely a global, salty layer of water.

Citation: McKay CP (2004) What is life—and how do we search for it in other worlds? PLoS Biol 2(9): e302.

Chris P. McKay is with the NASA Ames Research Center. E-mail: cmckay@mail.arc.nasa.gov

DOI: 10.1371/journal.pbio.0020302

WHAT IS LIFE?
ROBERT HAZEN

If we encountered alien life, chances are we wouldn't recognise it – not even if it was here on Earth

NO HUMAN discovery could have more profound ramifications than finding what's known in the business as a "second genesis" – an origin of life independent of that on Earth. With our present sample of one known living world, the possibility remains that Earth is unique and that we are utterly alone in the universe. But if we find a second genesis in our own cosmic backyard, then we will know that life is a universal imperative. The unproven conviction that the cosmos teems with life drives many of us in the nascent discipline of astrobiology – a field that one wit described as "the only science without a subject matter".

Earthbound biologists are exceptionally good at finding life. A single cell, a snippet of DNA, even an idiosyncratic collection of carbon-based molecules can point unambiguously to the presence of living beings, but those are signs of Earth life. What if life elsewhere is different, based on an exotic alien anatomy and biochemistry?

Unlike Justice Potter Stewart, who in his 1964 Supreme Court ruling on obscenity boasted some proficiency at recognising pornography, "I know it when I see it", I think the chances are good that we *won't* know alien life when we see it. So what exactly is life, and how can we detect it?

Scientists care about definitions, so they convene conferences to discuss the matter. A recent meeting called "What is life?" attracted a hundred scientists, who mingled with assorted philosophers and theologians to debate the issue. Opinions differed dramatically, but the most contentious debates occurred within the scientific ranks. One very senior expert on lipid molecules argued that life began with the first semi-permeable lipid membrane. An equally august authority on metabolism countered that life began with the first self-sustaining metabolic cycle. On the contrary, claimed several molecular biologists, the first living entity must have been an RNA-like genetic

system that carried and duplicated biological information. One mineralogist even proposed the decidedly minority view that life began not as an organic entity, but as a self-replicating mineral.

The unresolved debate was reminiscent of the classic story of the blind men and the elephant. Asked to describe the beast, each one's perspective varied, based on which feature was close at hand — the slender rope-like tail, the mighty tree-like legs, the twisting snake-like trunk, and so forth. Each man's version was wrong, but each possessed an element of the more complex elephantine truth. Perhaps the disparate claims of what constitutes life are likewise mere parts of the more complex truth of life's identity and origin.

Israeli origins expert Noam Lahav at the Hebrew University of Jerusalem underscored the problem of defining life in his 1998 book Biogenesis. Lahav tabulated a century of scientific definitions penned by 48 different authorities. The entry by the distinguished evolutionary biologist John Maynard Smith describes life as "any population of entities which has the properties of multiplication, heredity and variation". Alternatively, information theorist Stuart Kauffman claims that "life is an expected, collectively self-organised property of catalytic polymers". Other experts propose that "life is the ability to communicate", "life is a flow of energy, matter and information", "life is a self-sustained chemical system capable of undergoing Darwinian evolution". The definitions go on and on, and no two are quite the same.

Perhaps this should come as no surprise. Science is not the only profession to struggle with the question "what is life?". Bioethicists and theologians debate it in relation to the beginning of human life: does life start at moment of conception, when the fetal brain first responds, or when the unborn heart first beats? At the other end of the human journey, doctors and lawyers require a definition of life in order to deal ethically with patients who are brain dead or otherwise terminally unresponsive.

Scientific efforts to define life are less ethically complex and emotionally charged, but the lack of scientific agreement still represents an obvious problem. It's difficult to be sure you have discovered life on other worlds — or deduced the process of its origin on Earth — when you can't define what it is. In spite of generations of labour by hundreds of thousands of biologists, in spite of countless studies of living organisms at every scale, a general definition that distinguishes all imaginable living objects from the myriad non-living ones remains elusive.

What Is Life Becoming?

... life itself destroys beings.

Michel Foucault, *The Order of Things*

"Life itself" has long been a conceptual lure for experimental inquiry in the life sciences,[1] and yet its contours have transformed significantly since this singular phrasing appeared in the nineteenth century.[2] What Foucault named for that period as life's "untamed ontology"—caught between vitalism and mechanism—would appear by the mid-twentieth century to have been disciplined by techniques of mechanical and digital visualization. Molecular biologists came by then to claim that they had captured "life itself" in the form of high-resolution crystallographic models of DNA and proteins.[3] Writing in the 1970s, at the cusp of the informatics revolution in life science, French biologist François Jacob asserted this:

> Biology has demonstrated that there is no metaphysical entity hidden behind the word 'life.' The power of assembling, of producing increasingly complex structures, even of reproducing, belongs to the elements that constitute matter. From particles to man, there is a whole series of integration, of levels, of discontinuities. But there is no breach either in the composition of the objects or in the reactions that take place in them; no change in 'essence.'[4]

For Jacob, there was "no breach" in the series of links that tethered molecules to "man": The "essence" of life remained intact, from the atomic particles that make up matter, to the complex organization of the organism, and there was no need to invoke a special force to make sense of these phenomena. He broke with the view that "life itself"

1   On secrets of life, see Evelyn Fox Keller, *Secrets of Life, Secrets of Death: Essays on Language, Gender, and Science*. New York: Routledge, 1992.
2   Michel Foucault, *The Order of Things: An Archaeology of the Human Sciences*. New York: Pantheon Books, 1970.
3   See, for example, Francis Crick, *Life Itself: Its Origin and Nature*. New York: Simon and Schuster, 1981.
4   François Jacob, *The Logic of Life: A History of Heredity*. Princeton, NJ: Princeton University Press, 1973, p. 331; see also Richard Doyle, *On Beyond Living: Rhetorical Transformations of the Life Sciences*. Stanford, CA: Stanford University Press, 1997, p. 13.

was an enigmatic force and posited a fundamental continuity between inorganic materials and vital forms.

Rhetorician Richard Doyle explores this history to examine how a demystified science reconfigured "life itself" in the form of a molecule.[5] He documents the rise of a molecular biology that flattened living bodies into one-dimensional code. The new object of biological interest, deoxyribonucleic acid, came to be fetishized as informatic.[6] Such a view reduced living bodies to a kind of thinness and transparency, with nothing left lurking secretly beyond or behind DNA's codes. It was in the flatness of the rhetoric of "body as code" that the enigmatic force of "life itself" was simultaneously squeezed into a molecule and spread out into the thinness of legible text. With the helically coiled DNA molecule, life got unraveled, unzipped. For Doyle, this moment was marked by a profound ennui—emblematized by the possibility that a molecular geneticist could look down at the transparent body of a genome-mapped and cell-fate-mapped laboratory worm (*Caenorhabditis elegans*), shrug, and say "That's all there is."[7] Doyle suggested that a kind of "boredom" set in among scientists in genome projects: once "life itself" had been captured, the exhilaration of the chase had evaporated. In Doyle's reading, "the great unsaid of the life sciences, of a molecular biology that sought and found 'the secret of life,' is the fact that life has ceased to exist. Or, rather, it never did exist, that the life sciences were founded on an embarrassing but productive ambiguity, the opaque positivity called 'life.'"[8] By the late twentieth century, molecular biology had rendered the organism "postvital"; that is, "beyond living." Life's disenchantment was complete.

But what if the "untamed ontology" of the nineteenth century was never fully captured or contained? Evelyn Fox Keller has shown that a sort of vitality continued to lurk just below the surface of

5   Ibid.
6   See also Donna J. Haraway, *Modest_Witness@Second_Millennium.
    FemaleMan©_Meets_OncoMouse™: Feminism and Technoscience*. New York:
    Routledge, 1997; Lily E. Kay, *Who Wrote the Book of Life? A History of
    the Genetic Code*. Stanford, CA: Stanford University Press, 2000.
7   Doyle, *On Beyond Living*, p.17.
8   Ibid., p.10.

mechanistic theories throughout the twentieth-century life sciences.[9] She observes that geneticist H. J. Muller and his colleagues figured the gene as an agential "entity embodying the capacity to act within its own being."[10] Early concepts of the gene "betray[ed] a subconscious adherence to 'the ancient lore of animism.'"[11] Might a disavowed liveliness still linger in spite of the rise of putatively deanimated solutions to the problem of life?

Contemporary life scientists, I suggest, "do mechanism" in surprising ways.[12] The ambivalent renderings of the protein modelers and structural biologists with whom I have worked ethnographically, for example, hold mechanistic theories of molecular life that, it turns out, are rather "untamed."[13] The stuff of life does not resolve for them into fully deterministic machines. They figure proteins in registers that waver between the machinic, the human, and the animal. While practitioners may boast that they have captured and put "life itself" to work in the cell, they also simultaneously animate molecules as wily creatures who continually evade such capture. They show us that mechanism is not the hegemonic logic that would suppress the animisms and vitalisms of earlier life sciences. Rather, their work shows how the disenchantment of the life sciences is incomplete.[14] Modelers continually fail to contain the animisms and anthropomorphisms coursing through their renderings.

Could it be that the "postvital" apathy of late twentieth-century molecular genetics was just a passing phase? What if we paid attention to the affective entanglements of life science inquiry? Would we

9   See Evelyn Fox Keller, *Refiguring Life: Metaphors of Twentieth-Century Biology*. New York: Columbia University Press, 1995; Evelyn Fox Keller, *Making Sense of Life: Explaining Biological Development with Models, Metaphors, and Machines*. Cambridge, MA: Harvard University Press, 2002.

10 Ibid., p.217.

11 Ibid.

12 On the ways people may "do" bodies, see Annemarie Mol, *The Body Multiple: Ontology in Medical Practice*. Durham, NC: Duke University Press, 2002.

13 Natasha Myers, *Rendering Life Molecular: Models, Modelers, and Excitable Matter*. Durham, NC: Duke University Press, 2015.

14 See Vinciane Despret, "From Secret Agents to Interagency," *History and Theory*, vol.52, no.4 (2013), pp.29-44.

find a lively mechanism pullulating below the surface of life scientists' stories? My time with life science practitioners in their laboratories and classrooms has taught me that the contours of their ontology are so affectively charged that they are veritably *excitable*. What is this liveliness that continuously erupts inside of and alongside mechanistic descriptions of life?

Liveliness

Life itself is the psychic, cognitive, and material terrain of fetishism. By contrast, liveliness is open to the possibility of situated knowledges, including technoscientific knowledges.
—Donna Haraway, *Modest_Witness*

What if we were to make strange the idea that "life itself" is a thing that can be captured? The twentieth-century concept that life has an "itself" that could manifest in the form of a molecule should give us pause. Donna Haraway identifies "life itself" as a fetish object. Indeed, it is a ruse. To have an "itself," life must be pulled out of time and out of relation. "Life itself" is a lonely concept: This abstracted "it" is on its own; unresponsive and unaffected, left for dead. And yet. Twenty-first-century life scientists, it seems, are unable to resist hitching a ride on what Haraway might call the "unapologetic swerve of liveliness."[15]

Liveliness is not vitalism, and it is not the opposite of mechanism. Machines can be quite lively. Lively machines and machinic life are hybrid forms made possible through stories that refuse to make clean distinctions between the living and the nonliving, between the natural and the cultural, bodies and machines. These are the stories that articulate the subtleties and porosity of bodies in responsive, worldly relation with other matters and forces. Lively stories gesture at the unspeakable within the sciences, palpating the contours of sentiences beyond human and more-than-human worlds. These are stories that reach toward phenomena uncontainable by the colonial grammars of science and its calculating and extractive logics, intimating the sentiences of living and nonliving beings, including chemical and elemental forms. Lively narratives also subvert what colonial

15 Haraway, *Modest_Witness*, p. 137.

common sense would set aside as nonlife, what gets relegated as life's surround, full of exploitable resources for the living.[16] Liveliness is a relational concept.[17] It hinges on an intra-active conception of agency or *agencement*.[18] Intra-animating in dynamic contact improvisational choreographies, bodies of all kinds are open to move with and be moved by one another. In technoscientific contexts, lively stories irrupt from the kinesthetic and affective entanglements of inquiry that get practitioners intra-animating with other bodies and machines in their laboratories. In this sense, liveliness is a phenomena constellated

16 Elizabeth Povinelli, *Geontologies: A Requiem for Late Liberalism*. Durham NC: Duke University Press, 2016.

17 In some ways, this concept of liveliness is allied with the Indigenous knowledges of Turtle Island that are grounded in relationality and a recognition of the sentience of both lands and bodies, what Western ontologies still bifurcate into the living and the nonliving. This resonance may well gesture at an unacknowledged debt feminist theory owes to Indigenous epistemologies. For insight into Indigenous relations with more-than-human sentience see, for example, Robin Wall Kimmerer, *Braiding Sweetgrass: Indigenous Wisdom, Scientific Knowledge and the Teachings of Plants*. Minneapolis, MN: Milkweed Editions, 2015; Robin Wall Kimmerer, "Learning the Grammar of Animacy," *Anthropology of Consciousness*, vol. 28, no. 2 (2017), pp 128–34; Leanne Betasamosake Simpson, "Land as Pedagogy: Nishnaabeg Intelligence and Rebellious Transformation," *Decolonization: Indigeneity, Education & Society*, vol. 3, no. 3 (2014), pp. 1–25; Leanne Betasamosake Simpson, "Big Water," in Leanne Betasamosake Simpson, *This Accident of Being Lost: Songs and Stories*. Chico, CA: House of Anansi Press, 2017, pp. 65–68. For an experiment detuning settler common sense in the sciences of ecology to reckon with the sentience of the more-than-human and invent anticolonial ecological protocols that can ally with Indigenous land-sovereignty projects rather than exacerbate dispossession, see Natasha Myers, "Becoming Sensor in Sentient Worlds: A More-than-Natural History of a Black Oak Savannah," in Gretchen Bakke and Marina Peterson (eds), *Between Matter and Method: Encounters in Anthropology and Art*. London et al.: Bloomsbury Academic, 2017; Natasha Myers, "Ungrid-able Ecologies: Decolonizing the Ecological Sensorium in a 10,000 Year-Old Natural Cultural Happening," *Catalyst: Feminism, Theory, Technoscience*, vol. 3, no. 2 (2017), pp. 1–24, https://catalystjournal.org/index.php/catalyst/article/view/28848, accessed April 20, 2021.

18 On "intra-action" see Karen Barad, *Meeting the Universe Halfway: Quantum Physics and the Entanglement of Matter and Meaning*. Durham, NC: Duke University Press, 2007. On "agencement" see Despret, "From Secret Agents to Interagency."

through practitioners' intensive, prolonged entanglements with more-than-human phenomena in their laboratories and propagated through their stories.

Excitable Matter

"Protein folding is a deep problem." These words were repeated again and again by the lead instructor in a series of lectures I attended on protein folding as part of my research on pedagogies and performativity in life science classrooms. Why is protein folding a "deep problem"? What gives this problem "depth"? Part of what this educator was asserting was that the folding problem could not be solved simply with faster computers or improved algorithms. But it was not just that experimental techniques were not adequate to the task of rendering protein process in detail. Rather, his insistence was an affirmation that the *molecular practices of cells* evade complete capture.

The recalcitrance of the protein-folding problem has major implications for core assumptions in life science. One particular vision of cellular life, circumscribed by what practitioners call "the central dogma," has organized conventions in molecular biology since the discovery of the structure of DNA.[19] The central dogma, which hinges on an informatic model of the cell, dictates that complete information for life moves from DNA to RNA (ribonucleic acids) to protein sequence. This view of life has been a fundamental tenet in evolutionary theories which postulate that random mutations in an organism's DNA are the sole source for heritable variation.

University of Chicago biologist James Shapiro has explored the many "surprises" researchers have unearthed about "unexpected" activities ongoing in cells that would be "forbidden" under the model

19 For critical histories of the central dogma, see Keller, *Refiguring Life*; Kay, *Who Wrote the Book of Life?*; Doyle, *On Beyond Living*. For examples of ways life scientists are reworking the central dogma, see Enrico S. Coen, *The Art of Genes: How Organisms Make Themselves*. Oxford: Oxford University Press, 1999; James A. Shapiro, "Revisiting the Central Dogma in the 21st Century," *Annals of the New York Academy of Sciences*, vol. 1178, no. 1 (2009), pp 6–28; Richard C. Lewontin, *Biology as Ideology: The Doctrine of DNA*. New York: Harper Perennial, 1992; Craig Holdrege, *Genetics and the Manipulation of Life: The Forgotten Factor of Context*. Hudson, NY: Lindisfarne Press, 1996.

of life laid out by the central dogma.[20] These "complications or contra-
dictions of the central dogma" demonstrate that "there is no unidirec-
tional flow of information from one class of biological molecule to
another."[21] Shapiro's "short (and partial) list" of these "forbidden"
activities include such "epigenetic" processes as: reverse transcription,
which allows DNA to be produced from RNA sequences; posttranscrip-
tional RNA processing, which includes processes that can splice mes-
senger RNA and profoundly alter the message; the recent discovery of
catalytic RNA, which shows that some RNA molecules can behave like
protein catalysts and spur metabolic activities in the cell; recent discov-
eries that the "non-coding regions" found in the genome, those long
stretches of DNA commonly dismissed as "junk," do have functional
properties; epigenetic posttranslational protein modifications that can
transform a protein's cellular activities by the addition of methyl or
phosphate groups; and DNA proofreading and repair processes that
may be involved in directing specific changes in a DNA sequence.[22]

   If in the last half of the twentieth century, the central dogma
scripted genes as the primary actors determining the course of life,
new cellular actors are emerging for twenty-first-century life scientists. In addition to the menagerie of proteins that make up each cell's
"proteome," other molecules, including RNAs, are now hailed as
active participants in the story of *how cells do life*. One group of cell
biologists has made the call for a "molecular sociology" in order to
keep track of "who is talking to who" in the dense thicket of molecular interactions ongoing in a cell at any given moment.[23] According to
Shapiro, "biological specificity" does not have a "rigidly deterministic character"; rather, it obeys a "fuzzy logic."[24] The life sciences now
articulate the fine details of a story that does not just inquire into the
genetic determinants of life, but documents the *molecular practices of
cells*. These stories reconfigure cells and molecules as active participants in the *agencements* that shape their growth, development, and

20 Shapiro, "Revisiting the Central Dogma in the 21st Century," p. 7.
21 Ibid., p. 14.
22 Ibid., p. 7. On epigenetics, see Hannah Landecker, "Food as Exposure:
    Nutritional Epigenetics and the New Metabolism," *BioSocieties*, vol. 6,
    no. 2 (2011), pp. 167–94.
23 Carol V. Robinson et al., "The Molecular Sociology of the Cell," *Nature*,
    vol. 450, no. 7172 (2007), pp. 973–82.
24 Shapiro, "Revisiting the Central Dogma," p. 15.

reproduction. This new view of the cell and its molecular agents has implications for understanding evolutionary processes. Shapiro tests out a metaphor of "cellular cognition" to describe how cells actively sense their worlds and rework their biological activities in responsive relation to their environments:

> If we are to give up the outmoded atomistic vocabulary of 20th-century genetics, we need to develop a new lexicon of terms based on a view of the cell as an active and sentient entity, particularly as it deals with its genome. The emphasis has to be on what the cell does with and to its genome, not what the genome directs the cell to execute. In some ways, the change in thinking reverses the instructional relationship postulated by the central dogma. The two basic ideas here are: 1. Sensing, computation, and decision-making are central features of cellular functions; and 2. The cell is an active agent utilizing and modifying the information stored in its genome.[25]

Shapiro takes a bold leap to reconfigure the role of information transfer and the direction of its flow in cellular life. In this view, cells make use of their DNA as a tissue that not only remembers their evolutionary history but also records ongoing life experiences.[26] No longer a deterministic code, the genome can be seen as a materialized archive of memories left behind *in the wake of cells doing life.*

Cells in this view become sensing and sentient. Shapiro's formulation suggests that cells have know-how, an ability to respond actively and dynamically to their worlds.[27] And though he invokes the concept,

25 Ibid., p.23.
26 Mae-Wan Ho offers this insight: "In a very real sense, we never cease to write and overwrite our evolutionary history. DNA may be seen as a specific text in which organisms record their evolutionary experiences." See Mae-Wan Ho, "DNA and the New Organicism," in Johannes Wirz and Edith Lammerts van Bueren (eds), *The Future of DNA.* Dordrecht: Kluwer Academic Publishers, 1997, pp.9; 78-93.
27 See Lynn Margulis et al., *Chimeras and Consciousness: Evolution of the Sensory Self.* Cambridge, MA: MIT Press, 2011; Eshel Ben-Jacob et al., "Smart Bacteria," in Lynn Margulis et al. (eds), *Chimeras and Consciousness: Evolution of the Sensory Self.* Cambridge, MA: The MIT Press, 2011, pp.55-62; Evan Thompson, "Living Ways of Sense Making," *Philosophy Today,* vol.45, no.5: SPEP Supplement (2001), pp.114-23.

this is a model of sentience that reconfigures "cognition." It is an approach to sentience that might best be described by Maurice Merleau-Ponty's insistence that there is "a carnal adherence of the sentient to the sensed and of the sensed to the sentient," where sensitivity, the capacity to sense, is always already the promise of sentience.[28] Rereading Aristotle, literary scholar Daniel Heller-Roazen has described this relation between the sensitive and sentient as a kind of "inner touch" or "sense of aliveness" in things.[29] Cells are not just subject to their environments; they actively remake their worlds in responsive relation. Perhaps "How do proteins know how to fold?" can be understood within this context. How might protein folding be understood as a *molecular practice* in a cell that is actively sensing and responsively making its internal and external worlds?

Advocates of neo-Darwinism might consider this formulation blasphemous. A neo-Darwinian evolutionary view of the cell is beholden to the central dogma: DNA carries all the information for life; and it is mutations in DNA that generate heritable variation within populations. In this view, organisms are blind, mechanical actants driven by genetic determinants. Only those with the genes to economize their energy and maximize reproductive output survive.[30] An organism's genes determine whether it goes on to reproduce. Cellular events are deemed random and stochastic, even as advocates simultaneously figure proteins as deterministic molecular machines whose efficiencies are perfectly calibrated to their function.

And yet, as I have repeatedly encountered in my fieldwork across multiple life science disciplines, practitioners regularly defy their good training and deviate from these evolutionary scripts.[31] They describe plants, cells, molecules as if they were sentient entities with intentions and desires. It is by tuning into their often-muted deviations

---

28 See Maurice Merleau-Ponty, *The Visible and the Invisible*. Evanston, IL: Northwestern University Press, 1968, p. 142.

29 Daniel Heller-Roazen, *The Inner Touch: Archaeology of a Sensation*. Cambridge, MA: Zone Books, 2007.

30 For a fuller account of the economizing logics of evolution, see Carla Hustak and Natasha Myers, "Involutionary Momentum: Affective Ecologies and the Sciences of Plant/Insect Encounters," *Differences*, vol. 23, no. 3 (2012), pp. 74–118.

31 See also Natasha Myers, "Conversations on Plant Sensing: Notes from the Field," *Nature Culture. 03: Acting with Nonhuman Entities* (October 2015), pp. 35–66.

that I have been able to amplify the contours of a life science not so thoroughly bound to mechanism or neo-Darwinian logics. Their renderings manifest life as a relational phenomenon playing out in an excitable medium of wily matter. Theirs is not an ontology of vibrant things that appear to shimmer by their own light: liveliness is not an inherent property not of bodies or matter, but of bodies and matter in relation. Matter is lively and excitable for these practitioners in *ecologies of practice* that include both human and more-than-human practitioners.[32]

Openings

If liveliness is a lure for life scientists, it is surely also the lure that got me entangled with them in the first place.[33] My engagements with life scientists make no attempt to mask how I move with and am moved by their lively renderings. My rendering transduces modelers' pleasures and passions, their winces and cringes, along with my own. Transduction of course does not promise perfect translation.[34] Affects and gestures diffract through excitable tissues; signals get torqued as they are transduced. My renderings amplify some stories of life and life science practice, if not others. The aim is to challenge accounts of science that make it seem as if the capture of "life itself" is the only kind of story scientists know how to tell. Stories about such forms of capture are powerful lures that have drawn life scientists as well as their critics into their investigations. As stories told by scientists, narratives of the capture of "life itself" secure an image of the scientist's power over nature and model objectivity as disembodied practice. The effect is that such stories keep the life sciences locked into the logics of both neo-Darwinian mechanism and market forces. If observers of science only follow the scripts scientists think they are supposed to follow, we aid in entrenching and normalizing the hubris of stories of capture. We are complicit in limiting the kinds of inquiry

32 On such an "ecology of practices," see Isabelle Stengers, *Cosmopolitics I*. Minneapolis, MN: University of Minnesota Press, 2010.
33 On lures, see Isabelle Stengers, "A Constructivist Reading of Process and Reality," *Theory, Culture & Society*, vol. 25, no. 4 (2008), pp. 91–110.
34 Stefan Helmreich, "An Anthropologist Underwater: Immersive Soundscapes, Submarine Cyborgs, and Transductive Ethnography," *American Anthropologist*, vol. 34, no. 4 (2007), pp. 621–41.

and modes of attention possible in the life sciences. In this sense, stories told about science by those of us observing from a distance, which frame science as the capture of "life itself" for capital gain, risk reproducing the conditions that constrain what scientists can see, say, feel, imagine, and know.

How might we open up, rather than foreclose what it is possible to see, say, feel, imagine, and know in today's inquiries into life? Refusing the lure of capture, lively stories open up a wider discursive field to imagine life and the life sciences otherwise.[35]

35 For tactical conceptual experiments holding open what it is possible to see, say, feel, and know in the sciences, see on tactical biopolitics: Beatriz da Costa and Kavita Philip, *Tactical Biopolitics: Art, Activism, and Technoscience.* Cambridge, MA: MIT Press, 2008; Hustak and Myers, "Involutionary Momentum"; Carla Hustak et al., *Le Ravissement de Darwin: Le Langage Des Plantes. Les Empêcheurs de Penser En Rond.* Paris: Éditions La Découverte, 2020; see also Meredith Evans, *Becoming Sensor in the Planthroposcene: An Interview with Natasha Myers,* Society for Cultural Anthropology (July 9, 2020), https://culanth.org/fieldsights/becoming-sensor-an-interview-with-natasha-myers, accessed April 21, 2021. The interview discusses Myers' collaboration with dancer and filmmaker Ayelen Liberona (http://becomingsensor.com) in experiments at the intersection of art, ecology, and anthropology, which aim to invent protocols for an "ungrid-able ecology" uncontained by settler common sense or colonial ecology's economizing, militarized, and heteronormative logics.

CHEMISTRY & BIODIVERSITY – Vol. 5 (2008)　　　　　　　1

REVIEW

What Is Life?
A Brief Historical Overview

by **Antonio Lazcano**

Facultad de Ciencias, UNAM, Apdo. Postal 70-407, Cd. Universitaria, 04510 Mexico, D.F., Mexico
(e-mail: alar@correo.unam.mx)

Dedicated to the memories of *Leslie E. Orgel* and *Stanley L. Miller*

1. *'I Sing the Body Electric'.* – After many years of experimentation on the effects of electricity on frog legs, in 1791 *Luigi Galvani* published his *Commentary on the Effects of Electricity on Muscular Motion*, summarizing the observations that had led him to believe in the existence of 'animal electricity' that originated in the brain, and traveled through nerves and muscles. A child of the Enlightenment, *Galvani* was no mystic, and the fascination that his observations awoke in both his colleagues and the lay public (which are echoed in *Mary Wollstonecraft Shelley*'s masterpiece *Franken-stein*) must be understood as part of the process of secularization that life sciences underwent through this period: *Galvani* was, in fact, attempting to explain the nature of life itself on the basis of a purely physical phenomenon. As shown by the 19th century efforts to describe the basic properties of life on the basis of magnetism, surface tension, radioactivity, and other physical phenomena [1], *Galvani* and others had initiated a scientific trend that has continued for over two centuries.

In a way, *Erwin Schroedinger*'s famous book *What is life?* [2] can be seen as part of this trend. *Schroedinger*'s text should be read not as the starting point of the appeal that biological phenomena had over many physicists, but rather as the culmination of a long tradition that attempted to explain the nature of life in physical terms. What is generally not realized is that *Schroedinger* did not include in his book a single reference to biology. This is quite surprising, especially since many of his contemporaries were already having important insights when addressing basic properties of life such as heredity. A few years before *What is life?* was published, for instance, *John B. S. Haldane* wrote that '...*two possibilities are now open. The gene is a catalyst making a particular antigen, or the antigen is simply the gene or part of it let loose from its connection with the chromosome. The gene has two properties. It intervenes in metabolism, sometimes at least by making a definitive substance. And it reproduces itself. The gene, considered as a molecule, must be spread out in a layer one building block deep. Otherwise it could not be copied. The most likely method of copying is by a process analogous to crystallization, a second similar layer of building block being laid down on the first. But we could conceive of a process analogous to the copying of a gramophone record by the intermediation of a 'negative' perhaps related to the original as an antibody to an antigen...'* [3].

WHAT IS LIFE?
AMONG OTHER THINGS, IT'S A
SYNERGISTIC EFFECT!

Peter A. Corning, Ph.D.

ABSTRACT: There have been many different ways of characterizing and describing the phenomenon of life over the years. One aspect that has not often been stressed is life's emergent properties—the synergies that are produced when many elements or parts combine to produce distinctive new "wholes". Indeed, complex living systems represent a multi-leveled, multi-faceted hierarchy of synergistic effects that has evolved over several billion years. Some of the many examples of synergy at various levels of life are briefly described, and it is emphasized that life is still creating itself and still exploring its potentialities.

KEYWORDS: Synergy; Emergence; Evolution; Symbiosis; Hierarchy

Of all the wonders of the universe, life is surely the most wonderful. And complex. For living organisms have many unique attributes. Perhaps this is what accounts for our persistent difficulty in being able to define it in any succinct and quintessential way.

Over the years, life has been variously characterized as a "happening", a thermodynamic process, a repository (and a user) of information, a mind-boggling array of chemical processes, a complex division of labor, a robot vehicle designed to further the interests of "selfish genes," and many others. Life has also been clothed with various portentous buzzwords—autopoeisis, emergence, self-organization, sentience, autonomy, and more. And, of course, generations of philosophers and humanists, from Plato and Aristotle in ancient Greece to the 20th century paleontologist/priest Pierre Teilhard de Chardin—and many others before and since—have pondered the remarkable phenomenon of life in an effort to illuminate its essence.

We can perhaps date the entry of the scientific community into this dialogue to the Nobel physicist Erwin Schrödinger's legendary book *"What is Life?"* (1945), which was based on a set of his wartime lectures in Ireland. However, Schrödinger did not attempt to explore this ultimate question from a broad perspective. Rather, he advanced a reductionist claim about what he considered to be the most important physical property of life – its thermodynamic foundation. As a scientist with an interest in thermodynamics

Progress of Theoretical Physics Supplement No. 173, 2008   11

What Is Life? What Was Life? What Will Life Be?

David DEAMER

Department of Biomolecular Engineering,
University of California, Santa Cruz, CA 95064, USA

Our laboratory is exploring self-assembly processes and polymerization reactions of organic compounds in natural geothermal environments and related laboratory simulations. Although the physical environment that fostered primitive cellular life is still largely unconstrained, we can be reasonably confident that liquid water was required, together with a source of organic compounds and energy to drive polymerization reactions. There must also have been a process by which the compounds were sufficiently concentrated to undergo physical and chemical interactions. In earlier work we observed that macromolecules such as nucleic acids and proteins are readily encapsulated in membranous boundaries during wet-dry cycles such as those that would occur at the edges of geothermal springs or tide pools. The resulting structures are referred to as protocells, in that they exhibit certain properties of living cells and are models of the kinds of encapsulated macromolecular systems that would have led toward the first forms of cellular life. However, the assembly of protocells is markedly inhibited by conditions associated with extreme environments: High temperature, high salt concentrations, and low pH ranges. From a biophysical perspective, it follows that the most plausible planetary environment for the origin of cellular life would be an aqueous phase at moderate temperature ranges and low ionic strength, having a pH value near neutrality and divalent cations at submillimolar concentrations. This suggestion is in marked contrast to the view that life most likely began in a geothermal or marine environment, perhaps even the extreme environment of a hydrothermal vent. A more plausible site for the origin of cellular life would be fresh water pools maintained by rain falling on volcanic land masses resembling present-day Hawaii and Iceland. After the first cellular life was able to establish itself in a relatively benign environment, it would rapidly begin to adapt through Darwinian selection to more rigorous environments, including the extreme temperatures, salt concentrations and pH ranges that we now associate with the limits of life on the Earth.

§1.   Introduction

Could there be a connection between stars and life? Astrologers have always thought so, or course, but astronomers know better. Or at least they thought they did, until the birth of a new scientific discipline in 1996. The startling claim from Johnson Space Center scientists in Houston, Texas, was that they had discovered fossil microorganisms in a meteorite that was indisputably a chunk of the surface of Mars, sent sailing into space at escape velocity by the impact of a small asteroid. The excitement generated by this claim was not lost on Dan Goldin, the director of NASA. Goldin soon announced a significant new source of research funding, to be distributed under the auspices of a scientific program called Astrobiology. And that is how a seemingly impossible connection was made between astronomy and biology, by taking pieces of those two words, combining them into a new word, and most importantly, providing the research dollars in a competition that was certain to attract the finest scientific talent.

One of the goals of astrobiology is to discover how life originated on our planet

Биополимеры и клетки в измерении архитектуры микроценозов. 2. Параллельная жизнь; параллельная, но не жизнь; и непараллельная, и не жизнь, а что? Что есть жизнь?

В. А. Кордюм, Е. В. Мошинец

Институт молекулярной биологии и генетики НАН Украины
Ул. Академика Заболотного, 150, Киев, Украина, 03680

moshynets@gmail.com

Обнаружение образований, морфологически подобных клеткам микроорганизмов, с размерами от десятых до сотых микрометра поставило вопрос о теоретических границах того, что можно назвать живым. В этой связи анализируется представление о понятии жизнь и его применимости к различным идентифицируемым в природе пространственно локализованным объектам.

Ключевые слова: консенсус клетки, механизмы эволюции, самосборка, матричный синтез.

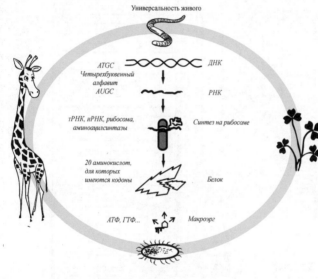

Рис. 2. Внутри клетки на молекулярном уровне все элементы консенсуса в своей основе универсальны и взаимоконвертируемы у всего живого. Такое взаимоконвертирование основано на принципиальной возможности взаимосовмещения элементов консенсуса. Но следует учитывать, что и совмещение, и конвертация «непрямолинейны». Их реализация требует определенных условий, которые в природе имеются

403

7

What is life?

7.1 How to characterize the living

It is a common understanding that it is impossible to provide a scientific definition of life which is universally accepted. This stems from the fact that the background of scientists dealing with the question – biologists, chemists, computer scientists, philosophers, astro-biologists, engineers, theologians, social scientists, ecologists (just to cite a few) – differs

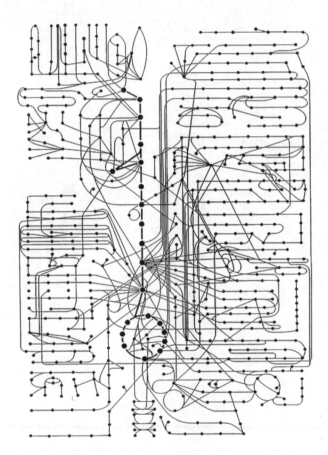

Figure 7.1 A section of the metabolic network of a "simple" bacterium. Note that each point (each chemical compound) is linked to any other point via the complexity of the network.

VIDA

¿ QUÉ ES ?

S U M A R I O

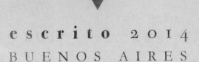

LA VIDA Y LA BRÚJULA
por **STEFAN HELMREICH**

e s c r i t o   2 0 1 4
B U E N O S   A I R E S

LA VIDA Y LA BRÚJULA

Cuando el Inspector Treviranus, de la policía de Buenos Aires, recuperó el libro de portada de cuero rasgada de genealogía de la mansión abandonada de su abuela en San Telmo, encontró perplejo una nota al márgen, un garabato, junto al nombre de Gottfried Treviranus, el alemán antepasado de quien había oído, una y otra vez, estos cuentos extraños y desconcertantes. Gottfried Treviranus, que vivió entre 1776-1837, había llevado a cabo experimentos, poco ortodoxos incluso para su propia época, sobre magnetismo animal. Hasta ahí, el inspector sabía. Pero la anotación sugería algo mucho más extraño - que Gottfried había creído, como tantos defensores de la teoría del magnetismo animal antes de él, en la proyección de la energía magnética a través del espacio (permitiendo que una mujer en Londres, por ejemplo, fuera "magnetizada" por un médico en Berlín que tan solo tenía un mechón de su pelo), pero también que las energías magnéticas podrían transportar fuerzas emanadas de seres vivos a través de la historia, permitiendo que organismos muertos tiempo atrás se manifestaran, o tal vez inc-

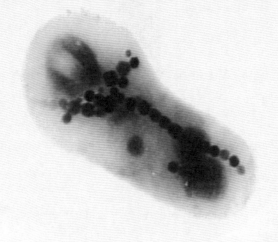

What is Life?

Guenther Witzany*

Telos-Philosophische Praxis, Buermoos, Austria

In searching for life in extraterrestrial space, it is essential to act based on an unequivocal definition of life. In the twentieth century, life was defined as cells that self-replicate, metabolize, and are open for mutations, without which genetic information would remain unchangeable, and evolution would be impossible. Current definitions of life derive from statistical mechanics, physics, and chemistry of the twentieth century in which life is considered to function machine like, ignoring a central role of communication. Recent observations show that context-dependent meaningful communication and network formation (and control) are central to all life forms. Evolutionary relevant new nucleotide sequences now appear to have originated from social agents such as viruses, their parasitic relatives, and related RNA networks, not from errors. By applying the known features of natural languages and communication, a new twenty-first century definition of life can be reached in which communicative interactions are central to all processes of life. A new definition of life must integrate the current empirical knowledge about interactions between cells, viruses, and RNA networks to provide a better explanatory power than the twentieth century narrative.

Keywords: sign mediated interactions, communication, cellular life, viruses, RNAs, evolution, essential agents of life, biocommunication

OPEN ACCESS

Edited by:
Tetyana Milojevic,
University of Vienna, Austria

Reviewed by:
Jordi Gómez,
Instituto de Parasitología y
Biomedicina López-Neyra
(IPBLN), Spain
Luis Villarreal,
University of California, Irvine,
United States

*Correspondence:
Guenther Witzany
witzany@sbg.at

Specialty section:
This article was submitted to
Astrobiology,
a section of the journal
Frontiers in Astronomy and Space
Sciences

Received: *22 January 2020*
Accepted: *17 February 2020*
Published: *18 March 2020*

Citation:
Witzany G (2020) What is Life?
Front. Astron. Space Sci. 7:7.
doi: 10.3389/fspas.2020.00007

INTRODUCTION

Scientifically, the first half of the twentieth century was the most successful period for empirically based sciences. Basically, explorations in physics and chemistry paved a path on which science could delimitate validity claims against all other concepts of thoughts such as the broad range of philosophical disciplines, theology, and poetry. Philosophers and physicists such as Wittgenstein, Carnap, Goedel, Russell, and Tarski suggested that exact sciences are strictly based on exact scientific sentences describing empirical facts coherent with observations and measurements in experimental setups (Wittgenstein, 1922; Carnap, 1931, 1939; Gödel, 1931).

The formal language to describe this was mathematical equations that would depict material reality. Information theory and cybernetic systems theory encouraged this progress (Bertalanffy, 1940; Wiener, 1948; Shannon and Weaver, 1949; Turing, 1950; Neumann, 1966). Milestone publication, "Principia Mathematica," outlined by Bertrand Russel and Alfred North Whitehead was further developed by David Hilberts axiomatic system with error-free logical sentences (Whitehead and Russell, 1910/1912/1913; Hilbert and Bernays, 1934/1939). This exact scientific language was applied to nearly all disciplines of scientific investigations in natural sciences as well as social sciences.

Molecular biology, genetics, and biochemistry started their success stories, which have lasted until today. The role of physicalism in biology was so dominant that biology became a subdiscipline of physics and chemistry (Brenner, 2012). Because biological organisms, cells, tissues, and organs consist of molecules, constructed out of atoms, empirical and measurable features may be described

Bulletin of the AAS • Vol. 52, Issue 6 (DPS52 Abstracts)

What is Lyfe? A Process-Based Characterization of the Living State

M. L. Wong[1], S. Bartlett[2]

[1]University of Washington, Seattle, WA, [2]Caltech, Pasadena, CA

Published on: Oct 26, 2020
Updated on: Oct 23, 2020

Motivated by the need to paint a more general picture of what life is — and could be — with respect to the rest of the phenomena of the universe, we propose a new vocabulary for astrobiological research. Lyfe is defined as any system that fulfills all four processes of the living state, namely: dissipation, autocatalysis, homeostasis, and learning. Life is defined as the instance of lyfe that we are familiar with on Earth, one that uses a specific organometallic molecular toolbox to record information about its environment and achieve dynamical order by dissipating certain planetary disequilibria. This new classification system allows the astrobiological community to more clearly define the questions that propel their research — e.g., whether they are developing a historical narrative to explain the origin of life (on Earth), or a universal narrative for the emergence of lyfe, or whether they are seeking signs of life specifically, or lyfe at large across the universe. While the concept of "life as we don't know it" is not new, the four pillars of lyfe offer a novel perspective on the living state that is indifferent to the particular components that might produce it.

What is Lyfe?

Dissipation

Autocatalysis

Homeostasis

Learning

Sub-Lyfe

Lyfe &
Astrobiology

What is Life? A Crash Course to Autopoiesis

From viruses to cognition, **Natalia Zdorovtsova** explains how defining life as systems of interactions can give new insight into its nature

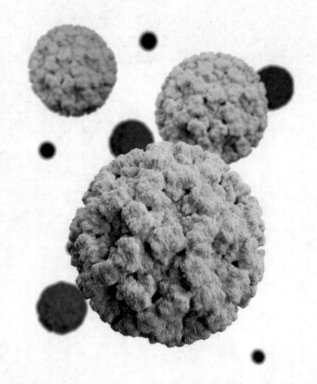

What exactly constitutes life? In the case of viruses (such as the norovirus shown above), biologists have tended to make up their minds based on the fact that viral replication depends on a host organism
ALISSA ECKERT/CENTERS FOR DISEASE CONTROL AND PREVENTION

This past year, we've heard a great deal of rhetoric that attempts to anthropomorphise SARS-CoV-2, the viral antecedent of COVID-19. This is best exemplified by PM Boris Johnson's insistence that the virus is an "invisible enemy" to be defeated and a "common foe" to all of humanity. This comes with a clear political intention — to resurrect a certain wartime mentality within the British public — but also raises an interesting question relating to the nature of viruses. To what extent can they be personified? And, indeed, are they *living*?

How Is Life?

It may seem self-evident that practitioners of the natural and biological sciences would have dominion over the question "What is life?" It may also seem obvious that the archive for posing questions about the question could be a chronological series of publications that take "What Is Life?" as their title.[1] Hoping to shake off some of the earnestness of the question—to make space both for playful experimentation and for those matters of life, lives, liveliness, livingness, and death that the query occludes—the speculative fabulations that we have distributed in this book aim to re-constellate the claims and investments made in the primary texts we have concatenated in these pages.

As it happens, the "What is life?" phrasing may itself already have overrun its expiry date and shed some of the authority that has followed from the seeming simplicity of its repeated enunciation. In a 2011 article titled "What Was Life?" one of our number, Stefan Helmreich, speculated on this possibility, describing the effects of reflexivity in the life sciences:

> Life moves out of the domain of the given into the contingent, into quotation marks, appearing not as a thing-in-itself but as something in the making in discourse and practice. Life becomes a trace of the scientific and cultural practices that have asked after it, a shadow of the biological and social theories meant to capture it.[2]

What might those shadows reveal? The times, places, and epistemologies that cast them. Consider the "life-sized model of a blue (or 'sulfurbottom') whale" that appeared in the American Museum of Natural History in 1907. As Michael Rossi (another Biogroop delegate) writes in his history of the model, the artifact was widely celebrated as a "close copy from life."[3] Here, life was sheer anatomical form, a

---

1 We thank Brad Bolman for his help in compiling this archive and Rodrigo Ochigame for activating a last-minute search across "all" languages.
2 Stefan Helmreich, "What Was Life? Answers from Three Limit Biologies," *Critical Inquiry*, vol. 37, no. 4 (2011), pp. 671-96, here p. 674.
3 Michael Rossi, "Fabricating Authenticity: Modeling a Whale at the American Museum of Natural History, 1906-1974," *Isis*, vol. 101, no. 2 (2010), pp. 338-61.

vision twinned with the taxidermic and taxonomic modes through which natural history museums came into being. Fast forward to Schrödinger's model of life as an effect of informatic organization, folded into compressed, coded form inside the organism, a vision that fit snugly into forms of life calibrated to Cold War practices of secrecy and cryptography. Move, next, to Lynn Margulis and Dorion Sagan's 1995 *What Is Life?*, which spoke to a world in which matters of biodiversity and of the biosphere—and their unknown futures—had begun to shape influential forms of planetary hope and worry.[4]

Theories of life often have implicit within them theories of history—and of temporality, of life pausing and restarting, slowing to a crawl (sometimes even reversing, reanimating), something Sophia Roosth (another member of our group) has detected in high relief among origins-of-life researchers, astrobiologists, paleobiologists, and other experimentalists fascinated with "latent" life (anabiosis, cryptobiosis, and other sorts of metabolic dormancy). In "Life, Not Itself," she argues: "the temporalities in which things move or do not move, and the speed at which they do or do not do so, is itself a principle by which things transition from organic to inorganic."[5] Evelyn Fox Keller has suggested that whereas "life" was once a diachronic question (life being the fleeting interval between that which is not-yet and no-longer alive), Schrödinger and modern molecular biologists pressed "life" into the domain of the synchronic—life as an all-at-once presence. In so doing, they placed life not in opposition to death, but to the inorganic. That secured the "What is life?" question as one delimited in the here and now, not the there and then. Yet, it seems that the *dynamics* of life—not "What is life?" but "what does life *do?*"—now command renewed attention. Geobiology, explored by a burgeoning community of scientists who study life as a geological force operating across millennia, is one scientific field reasserting a diachronic view of life.

Such a view also usefully queries the life/non-life distinction—a divide that has long subtended biopolitics as that which "brought life

---

4   Lynn Margulis and Dorion Sagan, *What Is Life?* New York: Simon & Schuster, 1995.
5   Sophia Roosth, "Life, Not Itself: Inanimacy and the Limits of Biology," *Grey Room*, vol. 57 (October 2014), pp. 56–81.

and its mechanisms into the realm of explicit calculations."[6] Biopolitics depended on a life/non-life division from the outset (hewing to the synchronic definition in which non-life is not death, but that which is inanimate, inorganic, or abiotic—unlively). In *Geontologies: A Requiem to Late Liberalism*, Elizabeth Povinelli critiques a stripe of vitalist chauvinism by arguing that social power has come to operate largely "through the regulation of the distinction between Life and Nonlife," a case she develops by drawing upon Indigenous Australian contestations with the settler state over what might count as livelihood, relation to land, and the matter of being.[7] Michi Saagiig Nishnaabeg scholar Leanne Betasamosake Simpson shows how Nishnaabeg intelligence cuts right through life/non-life polarizations and hierarchies endemic to colonial science, extraction, and governance projects.[8] The politics of trying to fix the "blurry division between the living and the dead," suggests Mel Chen in *Animacies: Biopolitics, Racial Mattering, and Queer Affect*, can be contested by attending to the affordances, dangers, and possibilities of "animacy"—a "quality of agency, awareness, mobility, sentience, or liveness," which might activate attentiveness to the unpredictable and wily worlds of matter.[9]

A reinvigorated awareness of life as something necessarily embedded in time—a view of life in history—focuses attention back to *lives and their times*. The politics of who gets to live and how, therefore, also calls attention to specters of death and death-in-life, thereby bringing into view matters such as the half-life of radioactive waste and the effective immortality of plastic waste.[10] Such matters point to

6   Michel Foucault, *The History of Sexuality*, vol. 1 [1976], trans. Robert Hurley. New York: Vintage, 1978, p. 143.
7   Elizabeth Povinelli, *Geontologies: A Requiem to Late Liberalism*. Durham, NC: Duke University Press, 2016.
8   Leanne Betasamosake Simpson, "Land as Pedagogy: Nishnaabeg Intelligence and Rebellious Transformation," *Decolonization: Indigeneity, Education & Society*, vol. 3, no. 3 (2014), pp. 1–25, https://jps.library.utoronto.ca/index.php/des/article/view/22170, accessed April 23, 2021.
9   Mel Y. Chen, *Animacies: Biopolitics, Racial Mattering, and Queer Affect*. Durham, NC: Duke University Press, 2012.
10   Max Liboiron, *Pollution is Colonialism*. Durham, NC: Duke University Press, 2021.

the productive, quiescent, active—and sometimes toxic—worldmaking elements that shape the narrative force of what Natasha Myers (another co-conspirator in our group) theorizes as *liveliness*, a *becoming with* (to borrow a term from Donna Haraway)[11] in which life and death are always entangled.[12]

Such an observation animates the work of Sara Wylie, who urges attention to how industrial and synthetic chemistry leads us to recognize "a biocultural inheritance that ties together human and environmental health by potentially transforming the biology of future generations."[13] Looking back historically at the object of biology also requires an epistemic shift: Hannah Landecker, for example, points to the necessity of understanding not just "the history of biology," but also the "biology of history," by which she means how historical processes such as the industrialization of food, the rise of antibiotics, endocrine disruption, and more have infiltrated not just the materiality of flesh, bodies, and ecologies, but also what has counted as the very matter of "life" that biologists have taken to be their subject.[14]

This lesson extends to how science has specified the idea of the "environment." In "What Was an Environment?" Etienne Benson notes that to many observers, systems models of the environment "seem to evacuate agency, experience, and embodiment, from our understanding of life."[15] Such scientific models, taken as formalist fetishes, provide an inadequate frame for apprehending the full politics of such claims as "Water Is Life" made by the Anishinaabe Women Water Protectors and other Indigenous advocates and allies. During the 2016 protests against the Dakota Access Pipeline that threatened to cut across Turtle Island (known to settlers as North

11 Donna Haraway, *When Species Meet*. Minneapolis, MN: University of Minnesota Press, 2008, p. 244.

12 Natasha Myers, *Rendering Life Molecular: Models, Modelers, and Excitable Matter*. Durham, NC: Duke University Press, 2015.

13 Sara Wylie, *Fractivism: Corporate Bodies and Chemical Bonds*. Durham, NC: Duke University Press, 2018, p. 16.

14 Hannah Landecker, "Antibiotic Resistance and the Biology of History," *Body & Society*, vol. 2, no. 4 (2016), pp. 19–52.

15 Etienne Benson, *Surroundings: A History of Environments and Environmentalisms*. Chicago, IL: University of Chicago Press, 2020, p. 5.

America), the Water Protectors made plain the thinness of the question "What is life?" when it is posed only from the vantage of biology.[16] A different kind of archive would and could emerge if the question were not "what" life is, but *which, and whose lives matter,* when, where, how, and in what relations—to water (from oceans to rivers to drinking water), to air (from atmospheres to medical oxygen), to earth (from soil to forests), and so on.

The "What is life?" question, as asked from the life sciences, then, is both too restricted and too full of unacknowledged investments in disciplinary and knowledge boundaries that often cut off questions of value by singularizing life, rather than speaking of *lives.* To fixate on questioning the "what" of life risks uncritically rehearsing biology's theories without also acknowledging how those theories have figured as rationales for racism (via, for example, typological classification), sexism (via, for example, fixation on reproductive substance as organismic essence), and colonialism (via, for example, abstractions of life from place). Even as biology is full of surprising, revelatory, and sometimes surreal or even funny stories that disrupt entrenched ideas about what life is and does (look, to begin, in our archive here), technoscientific practice has also often isolated, reduced, and mechanized living beings and their worlds to get at their matter and functions.[17]

The question "What is life?," therefore, can also often demand an answer in terms of a minimum, in terms of what Giorgio Agamben called "bare life," a figuration of the living that, as Alexander Weheliye argues in *Habeas Viscus: Racializing Assemblages, Biopolitics, and Black Feminist Theories of the Human,* has been underwritten by notions of the "primitive" and shot through with histories of ranking

---

16 Winona LaDuke, "No Line 3 Water Is Life," on the Honor the Earth channel [video], YouTube (uploaded August 13, 2019), https://www.youtube.com/watch?v=loYFNiee7wQ, accessed April 23, 2021.

17 See Sophia Roosth, *Synthetic: How Life Got Made.* Chicago, IL: University of Chicago Press, 2017. For a collection of practitioner views (some reductionist, some not) on how and whether "life" may be defined, see also Sandra Fernau et al., "What Is (Synthetic) Life? Basic Concepts of Life in Synthetic Biology," *PLoS ONE,* vol. 15, no. 7 (2020), https://doi.org/10.1371/journal.pone.0235808, accessed May 20, 2021.

peoples, ancestries, generations, races.[18] To tarry with "minimal life" is to tarry with the killable, with what Achille Mbembe has called *necropolitics*, the designation of some forms of life as outside ethical consideration.[19] This is the kind of framing that demands both resistance and a response that reasserts the multiplicity and significance of *lives*. As Alexis Pauline Gumbs puts it, "Police brutality, the destruction of the physical environment, the theft of resources from the so-called developing world, and every other horror of our time are based on a dominant and now-totalizing understanding of *what life is*, a poetics of the possible."[20] In this regard, Katherine McKittrick refashions "life" into "livingness," a term she deploys in order to eschew "a biocentric knowledge system and conception [...] that posits a Darwinian narrative of the human—that we are purely biological and bio-evolutionary beings—as universal."[21] This is a story that extends well beyond humans, too.

The "What is life?" question in and for biology has to some extent reached a point of semantic satiation, incanted to the point of glossolalia. Indeed, some astrobiologists have recently suggested that the notion of "life" is irredeemably parochial, and they propose replacing it with a concept they call "lyfe"—with "life" (as we know it) a subset process emerging only at some intersections of dynamics, listed by the authors as: dissipative, autocatalytic, homeostatic, and

---

18 Alexander Weheliye, *Habeas Viscus: Racializing Assemblages, Biopolitics, and Black Feminist Theories of the Human*. Durham, NC: Duke University Press, 2014. See also Giorgio Agamben, *Homo Sacer: Sovereign Power and Bare Life*, trans. Daniel Heller-Roazen. Stanford, CA: Stanford University Press, 1998.

19 Achille Mbembe, *Necropolitics*. Durham, NC: Duke University Press, 2019.

20 Alexis Pauline Gumbs, *Dub: Finding Ceremony*. Durham, NC: Duke University Press, 2020, p. x.

21 Katherine McKittrick, *Dear Science and Other Stories*. Durham, NC: Duke University Press, 2021, p.126. See also Katherine McKittrick, "Mathematics Black Life," *The Black Scholar*, vol.44, no.2 (2014), pp.16–28.

learning.[22] Such thinking doubles down on abstracting living things from their contexts, rather than redoubling efforts to reinvigorate life, liveliness, or livingness as active, mutable categories. That being said, the "lyfe" move indicates that the "What is life?" question may have been exhausted as much amongst scientists as humanists. In short, it has been revealed in both quarters as only one particular way of asking about origins, embodiments, relations, and futures. At a moment of bio-planetary reckoning—with pandemic, climatic, racial, and migratory transformations unevenly unfurling life and death across the globe—the sciences of life need revised queries, claims, and refrains.

22 Stuart Bartlett and Michael L. Wong, "Defining Lyfe in the Universe: From Three Privileged Functions to Four Pillars," *Life* vol. 10, no. 4 (2020), p. 42. The authors clarify that "lyfe" is pronounced "loif," diffusing any "Why is life?" English language/pronunciation wordplay we may have had in mind (though see Roosth's mention [this volume] of the "Warum Leben?" sign under a stromatolite featured in the Naturhistorisches Museum Wien).

A Chronological Select Bibliography for "What Is Life?"

p. 15   Henry Robyn, "What Is Life?," Sheet Music. St. Louis, MD: Bollman and Schatzman, 1867, title page.

p. 16   Anon., "What Is Life?," *Scientific American*, vol. 38, no. 18 (1878), pp. 272–73.

p. 17   Julien Pioger, "Conception expérimentale de la vie: Qu'est-ce que la vie?," *La Revue Socialiste*, vol. 15, no. 89 (1892), pp. 538–50, here p. 538.

p. 18   X. Y., *What Is Life?*. Toronto: The Copp, Clark Co. Limited, 1895, p. 11.

p. 20   Anon., "What Is Life? A Discovery by Prof. Gates, of Washington, which Answers the Question. An Interesting Subject," *New York Times*, December 7, 1897.

p. 20   Anon., "What Is Life?," *Lawrence Daily Journal*, March 1, 1898.

p. 21   Frederick Hovenden, *What Is Life? Or Where Are We? What Are We? Whence Did We Come? And Whither Do We Go?*, 2nd ed. London: Chapman & Hall, Ltd, 1899, jacket and p. 4.

p. 23   Joseph LeConte, "What Is Life?," *Science*, vol. 13, no. 338 (1901), pp. 991–92, here p. 991.

p. 24   F. J. Allen, "What is Life?," *Birmingham Natural History and Philosophical Society*, vol. 11 (1902), pp. 44–67, here p. 44.

p. 25   Justus Gaule, "What Is Life?," *The American Journal of Psychology*, vol. 14, no. 1 (1903), pp. 1–11, here p. 1.

p. 26   Oliver Lodge, "What Is Life?," *North American Review*, vol. 190, no. 582 (1905), pp. 661–69, here p. 661.

p. 47   Luis Razetti, *¿Qué es la vida?*. Caracas: Imprenta Nacional, 1907, title page and p. 265.

p. 49   Peter F. Swing, *What is Life?*. Cincinnati, OH: Roessler Bros, 1908, p. 5.

p. 50   Bertram C. A. Windle, *What Is Life? A Study of Vitalism and Neo-Vitalism*. London: Sands, 1908, title page and p. 28.

p. 52   William Thomson, *What Is Physical Life? Its Origin and Nature*. New York: Dodd, Mead and Company, 1909, title page.

p. 53   Edmund Ferrier, "What Is Life on Mars Like?," *North American Review*, vol. 197, no. 686 (1913), pp. 105–11, here p. 105.

p. 54   Eugenio Rignano, *Che cos' è la vita?*. Bologna: Zanicelli, 1925, n. p.

p. 55   Beverly L. Clarke, "What Is Life?," *Scientific American*, vol. 134, no. 2 (1926), pp. 82–83, here p. 82.

p. 56   William Patten, *What Is Life? Where is It? How is It Manifest? What Does It Signify?*. Hanover, NH: Dartmouth Press, 1927, p. 1.

p. 57   Augusta Gaskell, *What Is Life?*. Springfield, IL: Charles C. Thomas, 1928, title page and p. 150.

p. 75   Anon., "What Is Life?," *Nature*, vol. 124, no. 3124 (1929), pp. 397–99, here p. 397.

p. 76   Emma Reh Stevenson, "What *Is* Life?," *Scientific American*, vol. 140, no. 1 (1929), pp. 18–19, here p. 18.

p. 77   T. Swann Harding, "What Is Life?," *Scientific American*, vol. 156, no. 4 (1937), pp. 234–36, here p. 234.

p. 78   Erwin Schrödinger, *What Is Life? The Physical Aspect of the Living Cell*. Cambridge: Cambridge University Press, 1944, p. 5.

p. 79   John B. S. Haldane, *What Is Life?*. New York: Boni and Gaer, 1947, title page and p. 53.

p. 81   Walter Zöllner, "Was ist Leben?Der gegenwärtige Stand des Problems," *Zeitschrift für Philosophische Forschung*, vol. 3, no. 3 (1948), pp. 399–410, here p. 399.

p. 82   Hiroshi Tamiya, 生命とは何か / *Seimei towananika* (*What Is Life?*). Tokyo: Kōbundō, 1949, title page.

p. 83   Antonio García Valcarcel, "¿Qué es la vida?," *Medicina Española*, vol. 28, no. 165 (1952), pp. 485–96, here p. 486.

p. 84   Waldemar Kaempffert, "Reconstruction of Virus in Laboratory Reopens the Question: What Is Life?," *New York Times*, October 30, 1955.

p. 85   Lamberto Vitale, "Che cosa è la vita?," *La Rassegna di clinica, terapia e scienzeaffini*, vol. 54, no. 2 (1955), pp. 76–85, here p. 76.

p. 86   Karel Honzík, *Co je životnísloh*. Prague: Československý spisovatel, 1958, front cover.

p. 99   René Biot, *What Is Life?*, trans. Eric Earnshaw Smith. London: Burns & Oates, 1959, title page and p. 31.

p. 101   Daniel Mazia, "What Is Life?," in Colin S. Pittendrigh et al. (eds), *Biology and the Exploration of Mars*. Washington DC: National Academy of Sciences, 1966, pp. 25–40, here p. 25.

p. 102   Albert Delaunay, "Qu'est-ce que la vie," *Revue française d'odonto-stomatologie*, vol. 14, no. 5 (1967), pp. 685–95, here p. 685.

p. 103   Gerald Feinberg and Robert Shapiro, "A Definition is Debated: Exactly What Is 'Life'?," *Science Digest*, vol. 88, no. 2 (1980), pp. 52–57, here p. 52.

p. 104   Black Uhuru, "What Is Life?," Vinyl, 12". Jamaica-UK: Island Records, 1983.

p. 105   Martin A. Yuille, "What Is Life?," *Nature*, vol. 31, no. 7 (1985), p. 281.

p. 106   R. Lahoz-Beltrá, "What Is Life? Life as a Bioinformation System," *Origins of Life and Evolution of the Biosphere*, vol. 16, no. 3 (1986), pp. 324–25, here p. 324.

p. 107   Ernest Lawrence Rossi, "What Is Life?," *Psychological Perspectives*, vol. 26, no. 1 (1992), pp. 6–29, here p. 6 and 11.

p. 109   Evelyn Fox Keller, "Definitions of Life — Selected from the published literature (not exhaustive)." Compiled for "What Is Life?" panel at the International Society for the History, Philosophy, and Social Studies of Biology (ISHPSSB) meetings, July 1993, Brandeis University.

p. 119   Anon., "What Is Artificial Life?," comp.ai.alife, 1994, n. p. [archive online], https://usenetarchives.com/threads.php?id=comp.ai.alife&p=0, accessed May 19, 2021.

p. 120   Stephen Jay Gould, "'What is life?' as a problem in history," in Michael P. Murphy and Luke A. J. O'Neill (eds), *What is Life? The Next Fifty Years: Speculations on the Future of Biology*. Cambridge: Cambridge University Press, 1995, pp. 25–39, here p. 25.

p. 121 Lynn Margulis and Dorion Sagan, *What Is Life?*. Berkeley, CA: University of California Press, 1995, pp. 139, 33, 157, 175, 49, 67.

p. 122 Arnold De Loof, *Wat is leven?*. Leuven-Apeldoorn: Garant, 1996, composite.

p. 123 Josef Seifert, *What is Life? The Originality, Irreducibility, and Value of Life*. Atlanta, GA: Rodopi, 1997, front cover and p. 33.

p. 125 Curtis R. Naser, "What Is Life, and What Is a Machine? The Ontology of Bioengineering," *Critical Reviews in Biomedical Engineering*, vol. 28, nos 3-4 (2000), pp. 545-50, here p. 545.

p. 126 Douglas E. Dix, "What Is Life? Prerequisites for a Definition," *Yale Journal of Biology and Medicine* 75 (2002), pp. 313-21, here p. 313.

p. 127 Chris P. McKay, "What Is Life—And How Do We Search for It in Other Worlds?," *PLoS Biology*, vol. 2, no. 9 (2004), e302, pp. 1260-63.

p. 128 Robert Hazen, "What Is Life?," *New Scientist*, vol. 192, no. 2578 (2006), pp. 46-51, here p. 46.

p. 140 Antonio Lazcano, "What Is Life? A Brief Historical Overview," *Chemistry & Biodiversity* vol. 5 (2008), pp. 1-15, here p. 1

p. 141 Peter A. Corning, "What Is Life? Among Other Things, It's a Synergistic Effect!," *Cosmos and History: The Journal of Natural and Social Philosophy*, vol. 4, nos 1-2 (2008), pp. 233-44, here p. 233.

p. 142 David Deamer, "What Is Life? What Was Life? What Will Life Be?," *Progress of Theoretical Physics Supplement*, vol. 173 (February 2008), pp. 11-16, here p. 11.

p. 143 V. A. Kordium and E. V. Moshynets, "Biopolymers and Cells on the Level of Microbial Architecture: Parallel Life, Parallel but not Life, Nonparallel and Not Life, But What? What Is Life?," *Biopolymers and Cell*, vol. 25, no. 5 (2009), pp. 403-23, here p. 403.

p. 144 Fritjof Capra and Pier Luigi Luisi, "What is life?," in *The Systems View of Life: A Unifying Vision*. Cambridge: Cambridge University Press, 2014, pp. 129-43, here p. 129.

p. 145 Stefan Helmreich, "La Vida y La Brújula," *Falsch Sur*, 2014, front cover and p. 75.

p. 147 Guenther Witzany, "What is Life?", *Frontiers in Astronomy and Space Sciences* vol. 7, no. 7 (2020). doi: 10.3389/fspas.2020.00007

p. 148 Michael L. Wong and Stuart Bartlett, "What Is Lyfe? A Process-Based Characterization of the Living State," *Bulletin of the AAS*, vol. 52, no. 6 (2020), n. p. https://baas.aas.org/pub/2020n6i209p03, accessed May 17, 2021.

p. 149 Michael L. Wong and Stuart Bartlett, "Lyfe, A life, and Astrobiology, *Defining Lyfe in the Universe: From Three Privileged Functions to Four Pillars*, lecture, July 29, 2020 https://www.youtube.com/watch?v=AZ6u5ys1100, accessed May 17, 2021

p. 150 Natalia Zdorovtsova, "What is Life? A Crash Course to Autopoiesis," *Varsity* (January 22, 2021) https://www.varsity.co.uk/science/20521, accessed May 17, 2021

+   Katrin Klingan has been a curator at the Haus der Kulturen
der Welt since 2011, where she heads the Department of Literature and Humanities. She has developed and realized parts of
The Anthropocene Project (2013–14) as well as the long-term
research project *Anthropocene Curriculum* (since 2013). Recent
projects include *Mississippi. An Anthropocene River* (2018–19),
Life Forms (2019), and *The Shape of a Practice* (2020).

+   Nick Houde is a researcher for the long-term projects
Anthropocene Curriculum (2013–present) and *Technosphere*
(2015–19) at the Haus der Kulturen der Welt. Outside of HKW,
Houde has taught at various schools in Europe, including Bard
College Berlin, Zurich University of the Arts, and the University
of Applied Arts in Vienna, and is lead investigator for the Vertical
Union Working Group at the research- and network-platform
Trust.

Biogroop

+   Stefan Helmreich is Elting E. Morison Professor of Anthropology at the Massachusetts Institute of Technology. He is the author of *Alien Ocean: Anthropological Voyages in Microbial Seas* (2009) and *Sounding the Limits of Life: Essays in the Anthropology of Biology and Beyond* (2016). His essays have appeared in *Critical Inquiry, Representations, American Anthropologist, The Wire, Cabinet,* and *Public Culture.*

+   Natasha Myers is Professor of Anthropology at York University. She is the author of *Rendering Life Molecular: Models, Modelers, and Excitable Matter* (2015) and co-author, with Carla Hustak, of *Le ravissement de Darwin – Le langage des plantes* (2020). Her essays have appeared in *Social Studies of Science, Isis,* and *Catalyst: Feminism, Theory, Technoscience.*

+   Sophia Roosth is an anthropologist who writes about contemporary life and earth sciences. She is a Max Planck Society Sabbatical Award Laureate, and her scholarship has been supported by a Berlin Prize from the American Academy in Berlin as well as fellowships at the Radcliffe Institute for Advanced Study and the Cullman Center for Scholars and Writers at the New York Public Library. She lives in New York City.

+   Michael Rossi is Professor of the History of Science at the University of Chicago. He is the author of *The Republic of Color: Science, Perception, and the Making of Modern America* (2019). His essays have appeared in *The London Review of Books, Isis, Cabinet, Grey Room, Modes Pratiques,* and *The Tortoise,* among other publications.

+   Evelyn Fox Keller is Professor Emerita of History and Philosophy of Science in the Program in Science, Technology and Society at the Massachusetts Institute of Technology. She is the author of numerous books, including *A Feeling for the Organism* (1983), *Reflections on Gender and Science* (1985), *Secrets of Life, Secrets of Death* (1992), and *Making Sense of Life* (2002). She is also an elected member of the American Philosophical Society and the American Academy of Arts and Sciences.

Colophon

Das Neue Alphabet (The New Alphabet) is a publication series by HKW (Haus der Kulturen der Welt).

The series is part of the HKW project *Das Neue Alphabet* (2019–2022), supported by the Federal Government Commissioner for Culture and the Media due to a ruling of the German Bundestag.

Series Editors: Detlef Diederichsen, Anselm Franke,
        Katrin Klingan, Daniel Neugebauer, Bernd Scherer
Project Management: Philipp Albers
Managing Editor: Martin Hager
Copy-Editing: Mandi Gomez, Hannah Sarid de Mowbray
Design Concept: Olaf Nicolai with Malin Gewinner, Hannes Drißner

Vol. 11: *What Is Life?*
Editors: Stefan Helmreich, Natasha Myers, Sophia Roosth and
        Michael Rossi (Biogroop) in association with Katrin Klingan
        and Nick Houde
Coordination: Martin Hager
Contributors: Stefan Helmreich, Evelyn Fox Keller,
        Natasha Myers, Sophia Roosth, Michael Rossi
Graphic Design: Malin Gewinner, Hannes Drißner, Markus Dreßen
DNA-Lettering (Cover): Romy Strasser / Lea Fischlin
Type-Setting: Hannah Witte
Fonts: FK Raster (Florian Karsten), Suisse BP Int'l (Ian Party)
        Lyon Text (Kai Bernau)
Image Editing: ScanColor Reprostudio GmbH, Leipzig
Printing and Binding: Gutenberg Beuys Feindruckerei GmbH,
        Langenhagen

Published by:
Spector Books
Harkortstr. 10
01407 Leipzig
www.spectorbooks.com

Distribution:
Germany, Austria: GVA Gemeinsame Verlagsauslieferung
    Göttingen GmbH & Co. KG, www.gva-verlage.de
Switzerland: AVA Verlagsauslieferung AG, www.ava.ch
France, Belgium: Interart Paris, www.interart.fr
UK: Central Books Ltd, www.centralbooks.com
USA, Canada, Central and South America, Africa:
    ARTBOOK | D.A.P. www.artbook.com
Japan: twelvebooks, www.twelve-books.com
South Korea: The Book Society, www.thebooksociety.org
Australia, New Zealand: Perimeter Distribution,
    www.perimeterdistribution.com

Haus der Kulturen der Welt
John-Foster-Dulles-Allee 10
D-10557 Berlin
www.hkw.de

Haus der Kulturen der Welt is a business division of Kultur-
veranstaltungen des Bundes in Berlin GmbH (KBB).

Director: Bernd Scherer
Managing Director: Charlotte Sieben
Chairwoman of the Supervisory Board:
Claudia Roth MdB
Federal Government Commissioner for Culture and the Media

Haus der Kulturen der Welt is supported by

First Edition
Printed in Germany
ISBN: 978-3-95905-498-0

Recently published:
vol. 1: *The New Alphabet*
vol. 2: *Listen to Lists*
vol. 3: *Counter_Readings of the Body*
vol. 4: *Echo*
vol. 5: *Skin and Code*
vol. 6: *Carrier Bag Fiction*
vol. 7: *Making*
vol. 8: *Looking at Music*
vol. 9: *A Kind of World War*
vol. 10: *Re_Visioning Bodies*
vol. 11: *What Is Life?*

Forthcoming:

vol. 12: *On Image Systems*
vol. 13: *Artificial Music*
vol. 14: *Archives & Utopia*

ISBN: 978-3-95905-498-0

Spector Books